TAMING THE
TIGER

TAMING THE TIGER

FROM THE DEPTHS OF HELL TO THE HEIGHTS OF GLORY

The remarkable true story of a Kung Fu
World Champion

TONY ANTHONY
WITH ANGELA LITTLE

Authentic

MILTON KEYNES ● COLORADO SPRINGS ● HYDERABAD

Reprinted 2004 (twice), 2005 (six), 2006 (four), 2007 (four), 2008 (twice)

14 13 12 11 10 09 08   7 6 5 4 3 2 1

Authentic Media, 9 Holdom Avenue, Bletchley, Milton Keynes, Bucks., MK1 1QR
1820 Jet Stream Drive, Colorado Springs, CO 80921, USA
OM Authentic Media, Medchal Road, Jeedimetla Village, Secunderabad 500 055, A.P., India
www.authenticmedia.co.uk
Authentic Media is a division of IBS-STL U.K., limited by guarantee, with its registered office at Kingstown Broadway, Carlisle, Cumbria CA3 0HA. Registered in England & Wales No.1216232. Registered charity 270162

British Library Cataloguing in Publication Data

A catalogue record for this book is available from the British Library

ISBN 978-1-86024-706-4

Cover design by David Lund
Print management by Adare Carwin
Printed and bound in Great Britain

Dedication

I dedicate this book to Michael Wright, who called out to me in the wilderness and continues to call out to others.

Taming the tiger, defeating the dragon
(Chinese proverb)

And I saw an angel coming down out of heaven, having the key to the Abyss and holding in his hand a great chain. He seized the dragon, that ancient serpent, who is the devil, or Satan, and bound him for a thousand years. He threw him into the Abyss, and locked and sealed it over him, to keep him from deceiving the nations any more . . .
(Revelation 20:1–3)

Acknowledgements

This book covers a long journey and many people have played a role in its making.

Most of all I thank my wife, Sara, for her wisdom. She is my best friend, devoted encourager and most trusted critic. She brings balance, with a smile, to a deeply satisfying, yet sometimes emotionally draining ministry. And to my sons, Ethan and Jacob, who say, 'Daddy, we really miss you when you are not here,' and who remind me when I come home that daddies are for playtime, stories, kissing and cuddling.

This book would not have been possible without the tenacious devotion of Angela Little, the best co-writer anyone could hope for. There was an instant rapport from the time we first met, and her enthusiasm for this project has been unwavering and contagious. Thank you for accepting this project and seeing it through. Thank you for understanding the person that I was. Thank you for understanding the person I have become.

To Angela's husband, Phil, thank you for all your support and encouragement. And to their son, Samuel, who generously sacrificed so much time with Mummy. I am grateful to the many friends and family who have supported Angela throughout this project. Particularly, Gordon and Dorothy Little, Tony and Linda Smith and Chris and Linda McIntire for all the practical help and encouragement.

Thank you to Malcolm Down and the team at Authentic Publishing for your enthusiasm, courage and faith in this project.

Thanks to my Board of Directors, who have continued to give me guidance and direction for my ministry: Rob Land, Martin Eady, Sara Anthony, David Coleman, David Duell, Patrick Russell-Mott, Tina May, Jane Christian and Luke Dobson.

To my mentors: George Verwer, Steven Hembery, Gwyn Jordan, David Chadwick and Paul Wilcox, whose council and wisdom have guided and enriched my life and work.

And lastly, to you the reader. Thank you for taking the time to read my story.

Tony Anthony

Chapter 1

Shane D'Souza was barely recognisable. The guards scraped him off the cell floor and laid his mangled body on a dirty stretcher. He had been beaten, battered, cut, raped and ruined in every way. Pools of blood formed great purple patches on cold concrete. The trail of mutilation snaked its way down the dark corridor as they carried him off to the hospital wing. The small gathering of men shuffled away. We all knew who was guilty of the assault on the young Sri Lankan. No one said a word. The authorities didn't care. There'd be one less con – *fylakismenos* they called us – on B-wing. Another would soon take his place. There'd be no inquiry, no punishment for the attacker. No justice for my friend.

It was just another day in Nicosia Central Prison. We were murderers, drug pushers and smugglers, gangsters, child abusers, thieves, rapists, terrorists and fraudsters: a miserable mixed bag of human depravity; the meanest of the mean and the downright unlucky, tossed together in a stinking hot-pot of a Cypriot jail.

There were many rules, but they weren't the ones laid down by the authorities. We each lived by a code of violence, necessary for self-preservation. You always had to watch your back. It was every man for himself and blood was often spilled for little more than recreation. Still, there was something of an alliance between me and Shane. When I saw what had happened, it triggered a dark and dangerous rage inside me.

Al Capone – or 'Alcaponey', as the Greeks called him – was a nasty piece of work. No one knew his real name. He was one of the mentally deranged, the criminally insane. The courts didn't bother with asylums; they just abandoned their madmen among the rest of us. They were a law unto themselves. Alcaponey was one of the worst. A barbaric Cypriot, he was a loner, who barely spoke his own language. Serving time for murder and multiple rape, he was a grade one psychopath. Whilst the rest of us occupied our time with drug use, petty theft (primarily cigarettes and chocolate, which were the main form of currency), and occasional arts and crafts, Alcaponey spent his days mutilating and raping other inmates. He was a lifer on a mission to make a living hell for the rest of us.

On the day Shane was brutalised, I vowed his vengeance would be mine. Alcaponey was a good foot taller than me. He pushed weights and his arms were as thick as my thighs, but I knew I could have him. I knew I could kill him with my bare hands and make him suffer for every blow, every stinking sordid deed, every drop of Shane's blood.

In the days ahead, a hushed anticipation hung over the jail. Everyone knew I was after Alcaponey. It wouldn't be pretty. I was just waiting for my moment. Almost two weeks passed and with each day I grew more angry and ambitious in the suffering I would cause him. It wasn't enough to kill him. I'd make him beg for mercy, before releasing him to his devils. I was a world class Kung Fu champion, with the skill to burst him open and break him into a million pieces. I could do it easily, with my bare hands, but these days I often carried a blade. Most men did. We broke them out from our razors and hid them under our tongues or some other place where they could not be easily detected. It wasn't as though the guards bothered much. Some of them took sadistic pleasure out of it. Others just turned a blind eye. What did they care if an inmate got cut up or raped with a blade to his throat?

Gammodi bastardos!

Suddenly, I was slammed against the wall as Alcaponey's screech echoed round the dark, desolate corridor. I was angry at myself for being caught off guard, but adrenaline raced through my veins. At last, my time with the demon had finally come.

The stench of his breath was sickening as he leaned the full weight of his huge body against me, pushing his nose to mine. A blade dug sharply at my neck, waiting to slice my jugular. Immediately, I grabbed his greasy face with my free left hand, my thumb over his eye socket, ready to puncture. We grappled with each other, as I quickly calculated my moves. I knew I would receive a life threatening cut, but that didn't matter. Nothing mattered any more. I might die, but I would kill him first.

I wanted his blood. I'd easily take his eye, before ripping off his ear with my teeth. Fury boiled within me, but suddenly there was something else. In the heat of those split seconds I was strangely aware of a much deeper battle raging. It had little to do with Alcaponey. This one was all mine. It was as though some kind of new consciousness was weakening the ingrained instincts that made me the combat fighter I was. As I fought to focus my attention on Alcaponey's ear, I had an image in my head from something I had read only that morning. A man unjustly arrested, his friend defending him, cutting off the ear of the servant of his accuser. Alcaponey's ear was just inches from my mouth.

'Come on Tony, just bite. You're fast, you can take it,' the voice of my instinct spoke.

'No, wait . . . all who draw the sword, die by the sword . . . ' Where did that come from?

'Come on boy, just do it! What are you waiting for?'

As the conflict raged within me, I felt Alcaponey's free hand grasping down at my groin. His evil grin bared broken, rotten teeth as my fingers dug into his face, stretching and tearing at the leathery skin. There was the voice again.

'Come on, are you going to let yourself be cut and raped like Shane?'

What was stopping me? I didn't know. I kept a tight grip on the brute, as his body locked me against the wall, but something was preventing me from making my next move. The two voices of my inner being battled in the time it took for a drop of sweat to roll down Alcaponey's face, but it was as though time was standing still. It was a debate that addressed a whole lifetime and challenged the very core of who I was, who I had become.

I knew which voice had to win. But what then? Could I allow myself to be mutilated, just like my friend? Or could I really trust this new consciousness, this new voice that seemed so determined, so sure? Suddenly, words came out of my mouth. They were calm, clear, authoritative. Alcaponey knew only Greek, but in the surrealism of the moment, I spoke English. As I said the words, I released my hold and waited.

In the next split second I felt the weight of shock run through Alcaponey's body. He shivered and goose bumps rose on his clammy skin. His murky eyes glared in terror and I braced myself for the assault. Suddenly, my body heaved as he loosened his grip. We stood, still inches apart, glaring at one another's faces. Then, in a moment, he turned and fled. He was like a man possessed, running with his hands shielding his head.

His blood curdling scream bounced off the concrete walls as I watched him disappear into the darkness.

I put my hand to my neck and peeled the blade from my skin. It hadn't left a mark.

Chapter 2

I was four years old when the stranger arrived. People didn't come to our house, so when the doorbell rang I stood excitedly at the top of the stairs. My father let him in and showed him through to the living room. The stranger was Chinese, like my mother. I crept down to take a peek through the half-open door. They were talking in such low voices I couldn't make out what they were saying. From my hiding place, I could see the stranger's face. It was mean looking.

'Come in Antonio.' Mum's voice startled me. Being careful not to look directly at the man, I pushed quickly past him and tried to hide behind my father's legs. Mum reached out and pulled me to her. I didn't know what to do. I looked to Dad, but he just stared at the fireplace. He was blinking heavily, as though he had something stuck in his eye.

Suddenly, the stranger took me by the wrist. Flinching, I tried to pull away, but he held me tightly and Mum gave me that look, the one she used when I was to be quiet. She handed the stranger a small bag and, almost before I knew it, we were outside, walking down our garden path, leaving my parents behind.

I don't remember much about the journey. The stranger said nothing to me. I had no idea where he was taking me. When I found myself at the airport I began to tingle with a mixture of excitement and fear. This might be a fantastic adventure, but no, something was wrong, really wrong. The stranger still did not speak as we started to board a plane. As time passed, I grew more and more fearful. It seemed the flight was never going to end. Surely Mum and Dad would come soon? We'd go back to the house. Everything would be alright. Little did I know, I was on a plane bound for China.

At four years old I couldn't have understood the complexities of my parents' lives. What I did know, however, was my mother's hatred. Sitting on the plane, all I could do was think of her being angry with me. What had I done this time? I knew I had ruined my mother's life. She told me so. She was always angry.

Some time before the stranger came there was an incident I have never forgotten. We had moved from our little West End flat into a big house in Edgware, north-west London. To me it seemed huge and I remember squealing excitedly, running from one room to another. Mum and Dad bought a big new bed and I was bouncing on it, throwing myself face first into the soft new duvet. Suddenly Mum came storming in. 'Stop that immediately, you stupid child!' she yelled, dealing me a harsh slap across my legs. Moving over to the dressing table, she picked up the large hand mirror and started to look at herself, jutting out her chin, poking her lips and preening her eyelashes in the way she always did. I scrambled to quickly get off the bed but, in my haste, missed my footing and came bouncing down into the quilt once more. I couldn't help but let out a gasp of laughter.

Before I knew it, she was upon me. There was crashing around my head, an almighty cracking noise and my mother's voice, shrill, swearing and cursing at me. My head swam with sudden, intense pain.

'You idiot child, what did I tell you?' she was screaming in a frenzy. 'Now look at you!'

She marched out of the room slamming the door behind her. Somehow, I couldn't move. The frame of the

mirror stuck tight over my shoulders and pointed razors
of glass were cutting into my neck and face. There was
blood too, and more came as I winced in agony, willing
myself to pull a sharp edge away from my cheek.

I awoke with a start and realised we were getting off the
plane. Where were we? I tried to rub my eyes, but the
stranger still held my wrist. I wanted to cry. There was a
lot of chatter, but I couldn't understand any of it. People
were shouting, but their voices were high-pitched and
peculiar. Fear and confusion swept over me. Who was
this man? Where had he brought me? People scurried
around with bags, trolleys and parcels, but it wasn't like
the airport we had been in at the beginning of the journey. The air was thick with cigarette smoke and other
strange smells. Overwhelmed with drowsiness, I began
to cry, in big, breathless sobs. 'Sshh!' demanded the
stranger, sharply tightening his grip so I felt his fingernails in my flesh. My wailing was quickly suppressed in
pain and silent terror. He tugged again, this time pulling
me out into the evening air. It was then I realised I was
far, very far, from home.

    Like a frightened rabbit, I scanned the scene, hoping
to catch sight of my mother or father. The people wore
strange clothes. There was a lot of shouting and dogs
barking and a man with birds in a cage. We stopped.
Before me stood a spindly man dressed in a silky black
jacket with wide, loose sleeves and a high collar. Later, I
learned this was my grandfather. At the time, there was
no introduction. No smile. No welcome. I was hoisted
roughly onto his horse-drawn cart and, at the click of his
tongue, we pulled away into the night.

    As we left the airport behind I could see strange
shaped shadows of trees and animals moving around in
the half-light. I was terrified and felt queasy with the

stink that filled the air. (I was later to discover that it was the lily soap my grandfather used. It is very common among the Chinese, renowned for its antiseptic properties, but its odious perfume has always sickened my stomach.) It was to become the scent of my paranoia.

The journey seemed never-ending. When we finally came to a standstill it was pitch black. I could barely make out the shadowy surroundings, but I sensed there was a group of women standing at a gateway. Perhaps they were waiting for us. The women didn't like me. I felt that instantly. But what had I done wrong? My mind kept flashing back to my mother. Then, with looks of disdain and a crow-like cackle, the women were gone, all except one. She was, 'Jowmo', my grandmother.

Inside the house I shivered with cold. Still no one spoke to me. I wanted to ask where I was, but when I tried to speak I was met with a finger to the lips and a harsh 'Shush!' I was 4 years old and completely alone in a hostile, frightening world.

The house was very strange. I was shocked when suddenly a whole wall moved. The woman ushered me towards the bed in the corner. It looked nothing like my bed at home. Sticks of bamboo lay over a rickety frame. It creaked as I climbed onto it and pinched my skin when I moved. The thin muslin sheet barely covered me, but I tucked it round my shoulders, pulled my knees up to my chest and wept silently until sleep came. In the days and weeks ahead I quickly learned to stem my tears.

Each day began very early, around 4 or 5 o'clock. My grandfather (Lowsi, as I was instructed to call him, meaning 'master' or 'teacher') came into my room and beat me about the head with his bamboo stick to wake me. Soon I was rising before I heard his footsteps. I made sure I was up and ready to greet him. He hit me anyway. Lowsi's beatings were brutal. In the days and weeks ahead I got used to them, but they were always hard to bear. He used fresh bamboo cane, striking me over my ears, often until I bled. There was rarely any explanation or reason. He branded me *Lo han quilo*, meaning 'Little foreign devil'. It was his personal quest to 'beat the round-eye out of me'.

As my grandparents' only male grandchild, I might have been treated very differently. Boys in China are considered to bring good fortune and honour to a family and are often referred to as 'little emperors'. They are spoilt and doted upon by parents and, even more so, by grandparents. The problem was that my mother had married an outsider, an Italian, who was born and bred in England. She had brought shame on the family. It seemed I was to pay for the profanity.

Each morning I dutifully followed Lowsi out to the courtyard where he began his morning exercises. For several hours I shivered in my thin muslin robe but I hardly dared take my eyes off him, for fear of being beaten again. Sometimes I stole a glance up to the roof and the tops of the walls. They were decorated with the most bizarre things: dragons, phoenix, flying horses, unicorns and a man riding a hen.

At first I could only watch as Lowsi performed his strange movements. He made me stand very still and breathe deeply, in through my nose and out through my mouth. It was mind-numbingly tedious. As the weeks went by, and I began to pick up his language, he explained that his moves were 'Tai Chi', a discipline that is fundamental to the way of Kung Fu.

I quickly gathered that my grandfather was a Grand Master in the ancient martial art. He was revered by everyone in the village. That was why our house was grander than any of the others. I thought it looked a bit like the temple up on the hill.

Detail of my family tree is somewhat sparse in my mind, but I know that my grandfather originated from northern China. He fled down to Canton to escape the torturous atrocities of the Japanese invasion that extended into the 1940s. He was born into the Soo family, a direct descendant of Gong Soo, one of the so-called 'Venerable Five', who escaped the destruction of the original Shaolin temple under the Manchu dynasty in 1768. Gong Soo went into hiding and continued to practise Kung Fu. His knowledge passed down from generation to generation until my grandfather, Cheung Ling Soo.

As a Shaolin monk, my grandfather was proud of this 500-year-long heritage. Leaving the temple of his training, he began to develop his own styles and teach the ways of Kung Fu. He soon became a highly honoured Grand Master. Having no son of his own, however, meant the Soo lineage would be broken. I was his most unexpected and unlikely disciple. Perhaps it was for this reason that he would drive me to the harshest extremes of training. As part 'round eye', he knew I would have much to prove. In the years ahead, Lowsi would reveal to me the secrets and treasures of the ancient art. I would become a highly disciplined, truly enlightened disciple and an unbeatable combat warrior.

To become a true student of martial arts is to accept a whole code of living, unlike anything known in the western world. Its roots are derived from spiritual discipline and the practice of Taoism. According to martial arts lore, the father of Kung Fu was the Indian monk Bodhidharma. To the Chinese he is known as Ta Mo. Legend has it that he left his monastery in India to spread the teachings of the Buddha throughout China at the beginning of the sixth century. While wandering in the mountains of northern China, he stopped at a monastery called Shaolin. Shaolin means 'young tree', one that can survive strong winds and storms because it is flexible and can bend and sway in the wake of assault.

Ta Mo required that students be disciplined in the ways of meditation and the continual quest for enlightenment, but he found that the monks constantly fell asleep during meditation. He recognised that their bodies were weak and feeble, so he devised a series of exercises, explaining:

> 'Although the way of the Buddha is for the soul, the body and soul are inseparable. For this reason I shall give you a method by which you can develop your energy enough to attain to the presence of Buddha.'

These exercises were a series that served a form of moving meditation. They were also highly efficient fighting moves that helped the monks defend themselves from bandits when travelling between monasteries. Even so, Ta Mo's primary concern was not simply with developing physical strength, but with the cultivation of the intrinsic energy of 'Ch'i', perhaps most closely translated as 'breath', 'spirit' or 'life force'.

It is the development of Ch'i that lies at the heart of all the Taoist arts, including martial arts, philosophy and healing. Those early days in the courtyard, mastering my breathing through hours of practise, were to become the foundation of something extremely powerful.

One day Lowsi dressed me in orange robes and took me to the local Shaolin temple. The sky was a brilliant blue as we climbed the many steps to the entrance and a strange sweet smell hung in the air. 'Incense sticks and cherry blossom,' Lowsi said. 'We use them as a gift to pay our respects to Buddha.' Dutifully, I followed him as he lit some sticks on our behalf. 'Their therapeutic aroma will help calm your mind,' he explained. 'As you follow the path to enlightenment you will become like the smoke rising from the incense to the heavenlies.'

As my master led me over to a quiet area to begin our meditation, I couldn't help steal a glance at the monks who were combat training. 'They have bound their feet and lower legs with cords,' Lowsi said, noticing my interest. 'This is for strength and protection as they prac-tise their footwork.' I watched in utter amazement at the speed and power of their kicks. 'They are learning the way of the crane, one of the traditional Shaolin systems of combat,' Lowsi explained. I concentrated hard to follow his story: 'One day a monk stumbled on a battle between an ape and a crane. It seemed that the ape would easily break the bird in two, however, the bird had far more stealth than the ape. It flapped its wings and darted in and out with its beak until, at last, the large beast was driven away. Notice the grace in their move-ments,' Lowsi instructed, 'the powerful long-range kick and the one leg stance. See how the hands are used like the cutting of the crane's beak.'

As my training progressed I, too, mastered the way of the crane and many other systems of Kung Fu. Chinese martial arts claim as many as 1,500 styles. The imitation of animals is the classical and oldest Shaolin Kung Fu exercise. My master taught me that the human, being weaker than the animal, relies on his intelligence in order to survive. Yet to truly imitate the movement and mind of a particular animal is to master the physical art of immobility and rapidity, observation and reaction, steady movement and instantaneous attack.

'Now concentrate!'

Immediately my attention was snapped away from the disciples.

'Focus your mind on this flame.' Lowsi drew my eyes to the burning candle he placed in front of me. 'Centre yourself on the inner flame and clear your mind. Now breathe.'

We spent hours in the temple, staring into the flame of a candle. I longed to close my eyes, but as they grew heavy the thwack of bamboo hit my face. Lowsi beat me at any point he thought I was losing concentration. The purpose of these hours of meditation was to get in touch with the Ch'i. I was taught that all things are products of cosmic negative and positive forces, the yin and yang, which can be harmonised in the study of Ch'i. In the human body the Ch'i is best understood as the flow of energy. It is the Ch'i that disciples of Tao believe governs muscular movement, the process of breathing, the regulation of the heartbeat and the functioning of the nervous system.

'When you can completely harmonise the Ch'i in both body and spirit, you will reach enlightenment and inner peace. You will discover seemingly supernatural power within yourself,' Lowsi taught me. 'Harnessing the Ch'i is essential in the art of Ku Fu,' he continued. 'It allows for fluidity.' Dipping his hand into a small vase of water he held it in the air until a small drop formed and lingered on the tip of his forefinger. 'A single drop of water. Alone, it is harmless, gentle and powerless. But what on earth can withstand the force of a tsunami? Its raging waves have power to destroy earth and overcome all in its path. Learn to control the Ch'i, boy. Tap into its universal energy and you, too, will have power many times your natural strength.'

In the years ahead Lowsi's instruction in the Ch'i became clearer to me. I understood it to be the 'god within', the root of my power. Harnessing my body's energy through the Ch'i, I could break bricks with my bare hands and perform much more amazing feats. It also gave me a heightened state of awareness, to the point where I could sense the movements of an opponent in the dark and withstand immense pain by redistributing it throughout my body.

Everything about my life in China was intertwined in Kung Fu training. As a novice, I was made to do the most menial and difficult work relating to the upkeep of both our home and the temple. All the time Lowsi was preparing my body to begin training in earnest. One of the first exercises he presented to me was plunging my hands into a bucket of sand. Hour after hour I did this under his watchful eye, until my hands were sore and bleeding. After a few weeks, my skin hardened until I no longer felt the pain. Lowsi introduced small stones into the bucket and the procedure began again. Every few days he added larger stones until I was pounding my hands, with great force, into sharp boulders without cutting or blistering.

One of my main chores was tending the animals. My grandparents had paddy fields and we kept chickens, goats, cows and a horse. I was usually left alone to my work and I felt safe, away from Lowsi's harsh whippings. Among the animals I could momentarily set aside the pain of my training and the hatred I felt towards him.

Trips to the market with my grandmother were another welcome relief. I had to carry huge loads, but it was better than my master's merciless beatings. The market was noisy and colourful. People haggled and shouted to one another above the background rumble of the mah-jong houses. There were lots of live animals in cages: dogs, ducks, goats, rabbits, birds, reptiles and all sorts of strange fish on big wooden carts. I stuck close to my grandmother, afraid of being noticed by the 'reptile man'. He was very old and bent, with a wispy grey pointed beard, a thin moustache and a face that was creased like a dried up old prune. Long yellow nails stuck to his wizened fingers, and he used his sharply pointed thumb nail to cut up the throat of the terrapins he sold. On his stall were all manner of insects and snakes: live, dead, dried or skinned.

The medicine shop was another source of morbid fascination. Giant cobras were coiled in huge glass canisters and each shelf held row upon row of scary-looking jars filled with animal body parts, scorpions, beetles of all shapes and sizes, clusters of honey bees and snakes, all preserved in potent-smelling liquor.

Grandmother bartered for what seemed like ages with the herbalist. I marvelled at the huge chillies, brightly coloured powders and funny-looking roots that she bought to make ginseng and ginger teas. Back on the street there were delicious smells as people sat at the roadside, cooking in large woks. It was the 1970s and it seemed that much of Canton was under construction. Alongside the traditional shack-type stalls, giant western-style structures were being erected by barefoot or flip-flop clad Chinese, performing death defying feats on bamboo scaffolding.

We picked our way through mounds of rubble and pungent market waste, avoiding the constant pestering of people selling fortune-telling sticks. My attention was always caught by the calligraphers who set themselves up in the street with their brushes and inks. 'They use special xuan paper, made from bark and rice straw,' Jowmo explained. 'People hire the calligraphers to write letters for them and prepare special announcements.'

My grandmother could hardly be described as warm towards me, but she did seem to enjoy teaching me about the ways and traditions of our people. There are many festivals. New Year is the most important. The Chinese lunar year is based on the cycles of the moon and the calendar cycle is repeated every twelve years, with each year represented by an animal.

'Legend has it that the Lord Buddha summoned all the animals to come to him before he departed from earth,' Jowmo explained. 'But only twelve were prepared to come to bid him farewell. As a reward he promised to name a year after each one, in the order in which they arrived. The animals quarrelled over who should arrive first. Eventually, it turned into a contest. The first animal to reach the opposite bank of the river would be first in line and the rest of them would receive their years according to their finish. All twelve animals gathered at the river bank and jumped in. Unknown to the ox, the rat had jumped on his back and when the ox was about to jump ashore, ahead of the other animals, the rat jumped off his back and won the race, leaving the ox to come second. The others followed in the order of tiger, rabbit, dragon, snake, horse, sheep, monkey, rooster, dog and the pig, who was very slow and lazy, came last.'

Jowmo told me this story many times. She usually laughed out loud at the idea of the poor lazy pig. 'You were born in the year of the rooster,' she told me. 'The person born under the sign of the rooster is hard working and definite about their decisions. They are not afraid to speak their mind, but beware,' my grandmother cautioned, 'the rooster can be very boastful and overconfident. You will also be very brave,' she said, looking at me intently.

As New Year drew close, there was a great sense of excitement in the community. The twentieth day of the

twelfth moon was set aside for the annual house cleaning. My grandmother referred to it as the 'sweeping of
the grounds'. Every corner of the house had to be thor-
oughly cleaned. I helped her hang large scrolls of red
paper on the walls and gateway. In beautiful black ink
they pronounced poetic greetings and good wishes for
the family. We decorated the house with flowers, tanger-
ines, oranges and large pear-shaped grapefruits called
pomelos. 'These will bring us good luck and wealth,'
said my grandmother, as she carefully arranged a display of fruit. (In fact, this symbolism has developed
through a language pun. The word for tangerine has the
same sound as 'luck' in Chinese, and the word for
orange has the same sound as 'wealth'.)

'When the house is clean we will prepare the feast and
bid farewell to Zaowang, the kitchen god,' grandmother
told me. 'Tradition says that Zaowang returns on the first
day of the new year when all the merrymaking is over.'
There was lots of work to be done. All food had to be
prepared before New Year's Day. That way, sharp instru-
ments, such as knives and scissors, could be put away to
avoid cutting the 'luck' of the New Year.

On New Year's Eve the family gathered at our house.
They travelled from all over China and I was curious to
see my grandmother setting empty places at the table for
family members who could not attend. 'This is to sym-
bolise their presence at the banquet, even though they
cannot be with us,' she explained. I wondered if there
was a place for my mother, but I never asked. Many of
the guests treated me with the same disdain as my
grandfather, but at least there were some other children
– my cousins, all girls – to play with. There was also a
large lady with a big smiling face who winked at me mischievously. She was my grandfather's sister, Li Mei,
meaning 'plum blossom'. His other sister, Li Wei, did lit-

tle to live up to her name, 'beautiful rose'. To me, she was far from beautiful. She looked at me through the same shrew-like eyes as my grandfather. At midnight, following the banquet, the other children and I were made to bow and pay our respects to our grandparents and the other elders. I did as I was told, but I still hated them.

When New Year's Day came we were given red 'lai-see' envelopes. They contained good luck money. Everyone wore new clothes and my grandfather wore a fine red silk suit, intricately embroidered with an emblem of a dragon in gold thread.

I was quickly growing accustomed to my new life, but I soon worked out that, among these people, I would always be an outsider. In England, my mother had been proud of my oriental looks but, to the Chinese, I was very much a 'foreign devil'. I was 6 years old when I discovered that such prejudice, even in children, has no mercy.

One day, on the way home from the market with my grandmother, we stopped to rest by the village pond. As Jowmo lay back in the shade, I wandered around, casting stones into the water. Suddenly a group of boys not much older than myself surrounded me. 'Hey round eye, what are you doing here?' said one, spitting at me. In shock, I tried to understand what I had done wrong and what they were saying to me. 'He doesn't even speak our language,' scoffed another boy, giving me a sharp slap in the mouth. 'Come on, round eye, let's hear you say something.' I grappled for words, horrified by the taste of blood in my mouth. Then came another blow to my face. This time it was so hard that I lost my balance and went flying backwards in the mud. At once, all the boys were upon me, beating, slapping, scratching and dragging me by my hair. Fighting for breath, I screamed out to my grandmother but she didn't come. They kept on and on, shouting as they struck me. The noise of their abuse rang in my head until I began spinning in blackness, beneath the sharp blows of their kicks and punches. Then silence. No pain. Nothing.

I awoke in hospital, some days later. Both arms and one of my legs were cased in plaster. As I moved, a stab of pain ran through my whole upper body.

One night, whilst still in hospital and barely in a state of consciousness, I was aware of Lowsi and another man standing by my bed. I could only catch a little of what they were saying, but I gathered that they knew the gang of boys who had set upon me.

'Children of the Triads, from Shanghai,' the stranger said, 'visiting the local family.'

'They did not know who this boy is then,' said Lowsi sternly.

'Quite obviously not.'

'Am I to understand they have been dealt with?'

'Oh yes, the family has dealt with them most severely and the elders wish to meet with you tomorrow to seek your forgiveness and pardon.'

In the coming years the Shanghai boys were careful to stay away from me. Being from Triad families (the notorious Chinese mafia) they, too, were taught the practice of Kung Fu, but everyone knew that they would never receive the same level of training as me. Had they realised I was the disciple of the highly revered Cheung Ling Soo, they would never have dishonoured my family in this way and would have approached me in respectful trepidation. Such incidents are not easily forgotten among the Chinese. Years later the boys still lived under the weight of their childhood error. One time, when I returned to the village as an adult, after a period of absence, I learned that one of the attackers believed I had come back to claim my revenge. He was so scared that he was preparing to move his family out of the area.

Following the attack I spent many weeks in hospital, but I was barely free from the plaster cast when my master had me back in the courtyard, doing the most rigorous of physical exercises. The pain was so great that tears stung my eyes. This, I knew, my master would not tolerate. Sure enough, as a single droplet escaped down my cheek I felt the thrash of the bamboo across my ears. Hatred boiled up inside me. I was 6 years old but every fibre of my body, every drop of my young blood screamed out in loathing.

That night I woke in a cold sweat. I could hear the croak of insects and knew it was long before morning. The house was still and peaceful, but haunted dreams brought the frenzy of my hatred to fever pitch. Tossing and turning on my bed, I winced in the heat of fresh wounds. The image of my grandfather and his wicked bamboo cane tortured my mind. It would never end. But how could I stand even one more day? There was only one thing I could do.

As I padded silently through to the kitchen I felt the whole house would hear my heartbeat. Lowsi kept some of his combat cleavers in a large chest. We cleaned and polished them every day, so I was very familiar with the feel of them. I chose one and held it up, turning it so it reflected light onto my face. The blade was razor sharp.

A shaft of moonlight broke through the bamboo shutters and I could see my grandfather's sleeping form. I stood at a distance, looking at him, anger and repulsion sweeping over me like waves. Suddenly, I was aware of the heaviness of my breathing. Ironic that I would draw on his teaching to calm myself for silent strike. 'Focus on the Ch'i, concentrate. Control your body through your mind.' With my breathing in check I moved stealthily towards the bed. He was motionless.

I raised the cleaver above his heart.

Chapter 3

'Our Father, who art in heaven, hallowed be thy name
. . . ' It was a prayer my father had sometimes recited to
me at bedtime. He said he was Catholic because he was
Italian and God loves Catholics. But if ever God existed,
he'd obviously forgotten about me now. He had no place
in my brutal world. Everything about my life in England
was becoming nothing more than a hazy, confused memory. I couldn't even picture my father's face anymore.

Confucius taught: 'Peace in the state begins with order
in the family . . . The people who love and respect their
parents would never dare show hatred and disrespect to
others.' He also spoke of love, virtue and honour as
being the highest ideals in society.

I knew much about honour and virtue. These things
were beaten, quite literally, into every cell of my young
body. But love? What was love? I had never known it. I
was an unwanted child, a 'foreign devil' who brought
nothing but shame and bad fortune to those who were
supposed to love me. No wonder then that my 6-year-
old heart could be consumed by such hatred. It came
easily.

With the cleaver tight in my hand, I let the full weight
of my arm fall.

Then, an almighty force, like a rushing tornado. In a
flash, Lowsi's left hand sprang and grabbed the arm in
which I held the weapon. Twisting it up my back, he
seized me by the neck with his right hand, throwing me
to the floor. It was a move that I would learn and use

myself in the years ahead. This 'dim lo' technique is designed to immobilise an attacker in an instant. It is derived from a similar sister move called the 'dim mak'. Had my grandfather used this, he would have killed me.

Lowsi's fingers dug deep into my neck, cramming my head to the floor. I gasped for air but would have welcomed the peace of death. Looking back now, I might have detected a half smile on his face as his piercing eyes bored into mine. Perhaps this is what he had been longing for: a demonstration that, somewhere among the filthy foreign blood, there was enough Soo family spirit to secure the treasured legacy of the Shaolin fighters. All I knew then was the full weight of his anger and abhorrent hatred towards me. Dragging me by the hair, he pulled me out of the house, ripping off my clothes whilst screaming into my face that the lesson he was about to teach me would be like no other.

It was. I was severely beaten, then made to stand naked in the icy torrents of the river. It was one of winter's coldest nights and after several hours of pain I could remember no more. I awoke in hospital, suffering from hypothermia, with injuries that had taken me to death's door.

After that incident, something hardened deep in my spirit. I truly resigned myself to Lowsi's will. I was like a horse, finally broken and in submission to my master. I would become like him. I would earn his respect by being able to fight him as an equal. I became strong, focused and determined.

By the time I was 8 years old I had truly accepted my privilege as a disciple. As a novice I had been severely tested. Now, Lowsi was satisfied that I was fully committed to the way of Kung Fu. Now, he would begin to reveal the secrets of his heritage, as I simultaneously set my mind to the way of Taoism and to seeking the path to enlightenment.

My training moved up a level. We worked a minimum of eight hours a day, honing new techniques, building power, speed and strength. A large part of my daily training was with the 'mook jong' ('wooden dummy', or 'wooden man'). This piece of apparatus is a large wooden pole with protruding poles representing arms and legs at a variety of angles, ranging from foot to head height. It is usually either mounted on a frame, or secured to the ground by a heavy base structure. Lowsi had made his own mook jong by cultivating, trimming and carving one of the trees in our courtyard.

'Using the mook jong you will learn to sharply judge the angles and distances of your attacks,' Lowsi instructed. 'Always use the most efficient movement for your task.' I spent hours punching and kicking from all approaches, learning to engage and rotate at close distance to my opponent.

As a novice I had spent hours watching Lowsi make the traditional weapons of the Shaolin monks. He made blades of all shapes and sizes and part of my daily routine was to sharpen them using flint stone and oil. Being a Grand Master, my grandfather was in the practice of developing his own weaponry. As his disciple, I would become proficient in all.

Whenever we were out walking together we studied the trees in search of the ideal branch to make a staff or spear. We made a number of pilgrimages to a temple in Tibet. It was an amazing place, surrounded by beautiful willow trees, from which we could make long, perfectly straight staffs. Lowsi always carried an axe and we chopped the branches, cleaning them until they were smooth. They needed to be strong but flexible and I tested them by running at speed and vaulting with my full weight on the branch. 'Now watch carefully,' Lowsi instructed as he took one of the staffs and began showing me the techniques of the Shaolin fighter. With speed and stealth he moved through key block defence methods. 'Remember, a good fighter always concentrates first on defence. You must, at all times, be able to predict your opponent's next move.'

We trained with the eighteen classical weapons of the Shaolin, including clubs, spears, swords, tridents and whips. All were incorporated into my Tai Chi routines. Many of the weapons were used for exercise, to build strength, speed and agility, as well as for combat purposes. Training with the weapons was dangerous and I regularly sustained injuries. One day Lowsi presented me with two pieces of wood that were bound together by a length of rope. 'A basic nunchaku,' he announced. I watched as he performed his mastery, twisting the nunchaku around his body and flinging it with speed and accuracy at allotted targets. 'When launched at an opponent this can become a deadly weapon,' he told me.

I began using the nunchaku every day to strengthen my arms, swinging it over my head and across my body in the 'butterfly' technique. The key was to be able to manoeuvre the apparatus at speed, very close to the body without being hit. I was frequently caught at the back of the head and it was some time before Lowsi dare introduce me to the more lethal metal and chain version of the weapon.

I developed further strength and agility using the short handled clubs. These are ten-sided, solid iron objects of significant weight. Lowsi made me work with them for hours at a time. Frequently, he took me to the river to exercise in deep water, using the clubs in Tai Chi moves. 'Move your body as though you were in the air,' he shouted as I pushed against the flowing river. 'Focus your mind and evaporate the water's presence,' he called above the torrent, as I forced my muscles to maintain pace and vigour, against the water's heavy resistance.

I never questioned what Lowsi told me to do, and he continually pushed me to the limits of my endurance. He often left me alone to practise my exercises, but I never dared relax the intensity of my work. I had learned through harsh experience that there was always the possibility he was watching me at a distance.

One day he took me to a meadow quite near our home. It was a beautiful bright spring day, with clear blue sky. He handed me the clubs and told me to begin my moves. I worked until I began to ache. 'Continue,' was Lowsi's command, as he walked off into the distance. A great deal of time passed. Where was he? Was he hiding in the trees? I must not slow my pace. I continued hour after hour until my muscles burned and tears of pain began streaming down my face. At dusk Lowsi returned. 'You may stop now,' he said. He never offered a word of praise or encouragement, but I sensed that I was beginning to earn his respect.

Physical training was only part of my apprenticeship. To study the way of Kung Fu is to become fully immersed in its art and science. I studied calligraphy, languages and history and, from my early days as a novice, many hours were spent observing the behaviour of insects, birds and animals.

One day Lowsi brought a small wooden box out into the courtyard. The way he held it intrigued me, but at the same time I was fearful. He called me over and as I drew near he reached into the box with a pair of tongs. A scorpion. 'See how she moves,' Lowsi whispered. 'She is ready for battle. She does not like being touched or handled out of her own environment.' He held the creature in the air by its tail as it writhed. Then, he very carefully placed it on his open palm. 'She settles, but see, she is still alert.' I watched nervously. 'I must keep my hand perfectly straight and still. But remember,' he cautioned, 'there is energy in the hand. She must feel nothing.'

Transfixed, I held my breath. 'There is wind. See how I move with its breeze so that she feels no resistance in me,' Lowsi said. He held the scorpion for a few more moments then, with a flick, it was on the floor. I jumped back and felt the heat of a flush. He picked up the creature with the tongs and put it back in the box. 'Hold out your hand,' he instructed. I did as he said, but my hand trembled. 'Focus on your breathing. Lower your heart rate so you do not sweat. She must feel no pulse or moisture through your hand.' I concentrated and slowed my breath. This technique was starting to become second nature. By controlling my breathing I was learning to govern the workings of my body, so that I could disperse pain and alter my temperature at will. As I breathed, the panic began to ease.

Opening the box, Lowsi reminded me, 'Put your mind into hers. Release it from yourself. Become the scorpion. What will be her next move? What is she seeing? How is she breathing?' Placing the creature gently on my hand, he kept my gaze as I slipped into appropriate meditation. I remained perfectly still, but attentive to the environment of the courtyard. A sudden gust of wind or unexpected noise might disturb the scorpion and prove fatal for me. I longed for my master to release me from the tension. When he finally gave the command, my move to drop the creature was faster than lightning. Grandfather smiled to himself.

From the early days of my training I practised the art of putting my mind into that of an animal. This technique is essential to learning the many animal systems of the Shaolin fighters.

There was a praying mantis in our courtyard and Lowsi made me study its movement for hours at a time until I could imitate it. 'Tang Lang Ch'uan (Praying Mantis Kung Fu) was developed in the north of China sometime during the Ming Dynasty,' Lowsi told me, as we studied the creature one day. There was always some interesting history or legend to be learned about the different Kung Fu systems. 'It is thought that the founder of the system was the boxer, Wang Lang, over four hundred years ago,' Lowsi continued. 'Legend has it, he left his native Shantun Province to improve his Kung Fu at the Honan temple. But during this time he became disappointed with his level of skill. One day, by chance, he came upon a praying mantis in battle with a much larger creature. The mantis overcame the adversary and Wang took the insect back to the temple to study its movements. These he systematised with his previous knowledge, incorporating the erratic footwork of the monkey style, so creating the basic Northern Praying Mantis style.'

After his story, Lowsi began to train me in the Tang Lang Ch'uan system. 'The key move is the mantis hook,' he told me, forming my hand into the shape that resembles the insect's talon. 'It is used for striking, blocking and parrying.' He demonstrated some of the moves, making me blink at the speed of his five-sequence 'plum flower fist' staccato punches. 'Remember, the mantis' advantage is her silence, patience and determination. She is cunning and extremely efficient. She will often yield in order to conquer, so the emphasis here is on attack more than block,' said Lowsi. 'Using Tang Lang Ch'uan in combat you will strike from the elbow or the star of the palm. Aim to break the elbow joints.' As he spoke he struck a nearby tree with his mantis hand, slicing a branch in two with a single blow.

One of Lowsi's favourite techniques was Southern Snake Kung Fu. It is one of the most complex systems to learn and also the most deadly. Drawing on the influence of the viper, the cobra and the python, it makes stabbing hand motions to the face, throat and genitals.

'The viper inflicts heavy psychological damage by drawing lots of blood,' Lowsi told me. 'Its trademark is the tongue strike.' He positioned two of my fingers. 'Aim at main arteries and veins,' he said, demonstrating the stabbing technique in the air. Next he took my hand and opened it up, curling my thumb underneath. 'This position keeps a dynamic tension, characteristic of the cobra,' he said. 'The cobra concentrates its strikes on nerves and pressure points.' Lowsi went on to explain the way of the python, with its pinpoint strikes and grappling techniques. 'The snake is renowned for its speed and tenacity,' he warned. 'Once the reptile strikes, it hangs on and makes certain that its opponent will die.'

'A "dim mak" technique then?' I questioned.

'Correct. Ch'i is essential to the snake system,' Lowsi continued. 'It must be harnessed in your body in order to mimic a snake in its coiling and undulating motions. Only through Ch'i can the proper flow be achieved to allow the technique to work.'

One day, whilst grandfather and I were walking in the forest at the back of the house, I thought I spotted something moving in the undergrowth. My training had already taught me to be alert at all times and I had especially heightened extra sensory perception. 'The white tiger,' said my master, as though he had read my thoughts. His countenance was not the least bit altered and he continued to walk. 'She lives on the mountain. She has been tracking us for the last mile. Have you only just noticed?'

As we walked on, Lowsi talked to me of the white tiger, the way she lived and moved and stalked her prey. After some time we climbed into a tree.

'Watch. She will come eventually. She is curious,' Lowsi told me.

We sat in the tree for what seemed like an eternity. Then, through a small clearing we saw the exquisite markings of the rare and beautiful animal.

'Does she know we're here?' I asked.

'Of course. The question is, what will she do? Watch how she moves. Is she hungry? Is she playful?'

I studied the tiger as it padded furtively through the trees. 'She seems relaxed,' I said. As I whispered, the beast yawned and stretched, then settled itself among the ferns. 'Not hungry then,' I said with satisfaction.

'No, but see how she is always alert. She listens to our whispers in the air and smells our scent on the breeze. We pose no threat to her, so she is relaxed.'

I could not take my eyes off the animal. Transfixed by her beauty, I marvelled at her fine coat, perfect markings and the magnificent muscular strength and power that lay dormant but ready to strike in an instant.

In the weeks ahead we regularly tracked the white tiger. She never came near the town, but often ventured down to the forest at the base of the mountain. Sometimes grandfather laid fresh meat to draw her to us. I began working on my imitation techniques. 'You must understand not only the way she moves,' said Lowsi, 'but also the way she thinks, the way she breathes. You must be able to anticipate her. Only then will you master the tiger system.'

One day we tracked the tiger to a small clearing in the forest where she often went to rest and play. We deliberately moved down wind so that she would not detect our scent until we were quite close. As we approached she looked up from her nap. As if in recognition, she gave a small flick of her tail. Lowsi took his place, high in a nearby tree. No one could climb like him. I, too,

Taming the Tiger

began to scramble up the tree, but he stopped me. 'Go to her,' he whispered.

We had observed the tiger for many weeks at relatively close quarters, but I was all too aware that this was a highly dangerous, ferocious animal that could kill me before I could even think about it.

'She knows you. Move to her like one of her own. Become like her cub. Have no fear, or she will attack and you will die,' Lowsi instructed me. I checked my breathing and set my mind. Slowly and carefully I lay down my staff. With my arms down by my sides I tentatively began walking towards the beast. 'She must not see me as any kind of threat,' I reminded myself. 'I must keep my eyes fixed on the ground. Don't look directly at her face. Appear relaxed and unthreatening.'

Few people in the world have enjoyed the privilege of even seeing a white tiger in the wild. That day the mighty animal lay her large head against me and allowed me to tickle her ears like a common house cat. I glanced up at my master and smiled. Then, all of a sudden, there was the crack of a branch from his direction. Jumping in surprise, I lost my concentration and quickly pulled my hand away from the tiger. As I did she swiped at me with a mighty paw. Incredibly, I managed to pull away before she tore my flesh, but as I moved she came around with her second front paw to swipe again. The tiger was beginning to rise and I knew I was in trouble. I had to keep my head. Face down. Do not make eye contact. I fought the natural instinct to run, which would surely have had her upon me in an instant. Instead, I forced myself into the same passive stance with which I had first approached, keeping my eyes fixed on her paws and away from her gaze. She rose no further and, as I took a slow step backwards, she settled once more to lie amongst the undergrowth.

Lowsi greeted me with a bow. It was the first time he had given me this sign of respect. 'You are learning well.' From that day, he called me 'Lo Fu Zai', meaning 'Little Tiger'.

Of all the animals I studied, I found myself most drawn to the way of the tiger. As a Kung Fu system it was developed to empower the bones, tendons and muscles. The moves are short, snappy and forceful, with emphasis placed on strength and tension. The tiger is defensive in nature, waiting until it is backed into a corner before unleashing an unstoppable assault. In combat the tiger practitioner fights fiercely, tearing and breaking. With its tiger claw hand position, this system is very useful in unarmed defence against weapons. By clasping the weapon between the hands or enmeshing it in its crushing grip, the enemy's advantage is lost.

One morning, when I was around 10 years old, Lowsi led me out into the forest. It was very early and barely light. We walked for several miles, meditating, as usual, but this time we took a route that was unknown to me. Eventually we came to a wooden rack. As I studied it I saw that it was suspended under the thick branch of a sturdy tree trunk by a heavy rope which looped down to the branch of another tree. The rack was octagonal in shape and about 10 feet from side to side. It had hundreds of sharp spikes of identical length sticking straight down from its underside. My throat grew dry as I looked at the ground beneath the rack and saw that it was heavily scuffed with footprints.

'Get under the rack,' Lowsi instructed me. As usual, I obeyed him without question. Under the rack I looked up at the threatening spikes, shining in the dim light of morning. 'Assume the tiger stance.' I lowered myself as he moved the rope through his hands until the rack was centimetres from my body. 'Now get lower, until your thighs are parallel with the ground.' I obeyed. 'This is the flat tiger,' Lowsi told me. 'It is not used for fighting, but will help you strengthen your legs.' As he spoke he lowered the rack even more. 'Be sure that you do not raise up,' he said, and with that he walked away, back in the direction of the house.

I held the position for what seemed like an age. It was getting light and though the heat of the day was far from its full force, sweat was pouring from me. My legs burned with pain, but I dare not move for fear of the spikes. Then, as if from nowhere, Lowsi appeared. He walked slowly around the rack, checking my position. He could see my suffering. Tears and sweat were streaming down my cheeks. 'You can relieve yourself by sweeping one leg straight across the ground,' he told me. It was a hard move, but it did at least ease some of the cramp. 'This is a bow and arrow stance,' he told me. 'See how your forward leg is now bent, like a bow and the rear leg is locked into the ground, holding straight like an arrow.'

Lowsi taught me a number of flat stances using the rack. They were deeper versions of many of the tiger fighting stances I knew. A regular part of my training involved quick switching from the bow and arrow stance to the fighting cat stance, to the twist and through to the horse. During months of practice with the rack I learned how to manoeuvre in flat stances and my legs became knotted cords of rock-hard muscle. Lowsi also built endurance in my arms in this way. It was a cruel lesson, but as I lay under the rack, supported on my burning limbs, he would hand me rocks to hold in my hands. The pain was unbearable, but I could not, and would not, give up.

As time went by, many of these positions became second nature to me. I could assume them without even thinking. Lowsi would test me at any time. One night, he came into my room while I was sleeping and threw a bucket of iced water over me. I immediately leapt up into a fighting horse stance, without knowing what was happening. He was screaming at me about the position. 'Get that shoulder further forward,' he yelled as he slapped me. Then, in a kinder tone, he instructed me to prepare for my study and meditation in the courtyard.

Once outside Lowsi reached into a basket and pulled an expensive-looking inkwell, a fine set of brass quills and blank paper from beneath the cloth cover. 'I want you to write all that you have learned about the fighting tiger stance and technique.' The task was a welcome break from the physical endurance exercises, but I was left to sit at my work from early morning until late in the evening.

The courtyard had always been a place of misery and torture yet, that day, as I meditated alone, I began to see that it was quite beautiful. Looking out beyond the moon gate on the far wall, I studied the southern slopes of the Hanshan Si, the Cold Mountain. Squinting through the sunlight, I could just about make out the shape of its monastery nestled high above the Cassia forest. Above my head, mythological beasts danced on the roof and perimeter walls. They had always fascinated me. Now I knew they were believed to protect the building from evil spirits.

Like most Chinese, my family were deeply superstitious, yet the way of Kung Fu was giving me confidence to overcome any kind of fear. 'There is no god, only the god within,' Lowsi told me again and again. 'Use the Ch'i to conquer your fear.' Lowsi had many strategies to beat any fear out of me. Once we climbed a mountain for several days until we reached a terrifying ridge. In the middle of a raging storm he instructed me to begin my exercises. It was almost impossible to concentrate with the lashing rain biting into my thin clothing and the gusting wind bringing the threat of the mighty crevasse ever nearer.

Soon after this, Lowsi began arranging combat opportunities for me. We travelled to temples all over China, as far north-east as Shandong and Tanggu, across to Lanzhou and Chengdu, as far west as Tibet and occasionally across to Pakistan. I had been taught not to show any emotion, but I still indulged a silent tremor of excitement whenever we travelled to Hong Kong. It was the end of the 1970s and the island was vibrant with life. There were sports cars and men in smart western suits, with lights and music everywhere.

My first trip to Hong Kong was to attend the Kumatai. It was an illegal competition, although police and other officials were seen placing their bets with everyone else. 'The Kumatai is full contact freestyle competition. Practitioners from all systems of martial arts combat can pitch against one another,' Lowsi explained, as we took our place in the arena. It had a different atmosphere to any of the other competitions I had attended. 'They are bloodthirsty,' said grandfather as he noticed me looking around the frenzied crowd. 'It is not uncommon for a fight to end in the death of a competitor.' I knew that Lowsi had fought in the Kumatai many times himself. 'One day soon you will rule the Kumatai,' he told me. I knew he was right.

Chapter 4

When I was 12 years old, my grandfather announced that I was to be sent back to England. I was excited but, at the same time, daunted at the prospect of living with my parents. On the journey to the airport Lowsi and I sat in silent meditation. As we were nearing the terminal he explained that my training would continue in London. 'I have made arrangements through the International Kung Fu Federation in Geneva. They will approve a tutor and fund your training,' he told me. The cart drew to a halt. 'I will monitor your progress and you will return to me in time.' With that, he bowed to me and left.

As the plane rose into the sky I wondered what might lie ahead of me. I had made a number of trips home during the eight years I had lived in China, sometimes staying a couple of months at a time. I was always fascinated by the city. It was so fast and busy. I loved to see the shops full of toys, the punk rockers that hung around Trafalgar Square, the red London buses and bright lights of Piccadilly. But being with my parents was never easy. They refused to acknowledge anything about my life in China. Mum, especially, behaved as though I had never been away. She was always awkward around me. We didn't talk much at all. It didn't help that I struggled to speak and understand English. Cantonese had very quickly become my first language. Surely she, too, spoke the language of her ancestry? I never asked her about it. There was much about my family that I didn't understand.

As I settled into the flight my mind began to wander back to the last time I was in England, when I was 9 years old. One day I had gone with my mother to the supermarket. As usual, she crammed the trolley full of groceries and nice treats. I noticed that there was an expensive packet of king prawns hiding underneath her handbag, in the bottom of the trolley.

'Look, you forgot these,' I said innocently, as she unloaded the shopping at the checkout.

'Oh, silly me. Fancy that?' she said, looking embarrassed as she pulled the packet onto the counter and dipped into her purse for extra money.

'Don't worry,' said the checkout girl. 'It's an easy mistake to make.'

My mother was angry as we left the store. Her face was clouded with a tight-lipped scowl, but I was used to that. I didn't understand what had gone wrong, but I knew it was best to remain silent.

I might have thought nothing more of the episode, however, a few days later, the very same thing happened again. This time it was a luxurious box of chocolates. Moving towards the checkout my mother picked it out of the trolley and held it in her hand with her long coat covering the box.

'Mum, you haven't . . . ' I stopped. My mother's harsh look said it all.

Haunted by the memory, I tried to remember happier times. My mind went back to the early days when my parents were living in the big house in Edgware. Dad was a successful television engineer and his business must have been thriving. One night he came in shouting and laughing. One of his customers had paid him a large sum of money in cash. Bursting through the door, he flung the wad of banknotes in the air. Mum was beside herself with excitement and she ran, grabbing at them. I

watched in glee as Dad swung her up by her waist and
they danced around the room in celebration. It was one
of very few happy times I remembered at home.

The hours passed and I concentrated on the drone and
changing sounds of the plane's engine. Finally, I fell
asleep and was awakened just as we began our descent
into London's Heathrow airport.

The air flight attendants were always very attentive
and, after the plane touched down, one escorted me
through the terminal to where my parents were waiting.
I had no luggage to collect. The arrivals area was
crammed with expectant people and I scanned the
crowd looking for my mother and father. I soon spotted
them. My mother, as I always pictured her, in smart
clothes, bright red lipstick, heavy black lashes and
matching handbag and boots. The sight of my father
made me catch my breath. In my mind he was a tall, fine
looking man, with sharp features, olive skin and thick,
black, wavy hair. Now he was sitting in a wheelchair. He
appeared small and pale and his hair was peppered with
grey. I greeted them with a short bow. My mother, looking awkward and uncomfortable, gave me a sharp kiss
on the cheek.

I later learned something of my father's illness. It was
multiple sclerosis. He had been diagnosed shortly after I
was born. Perhaps that was the reason my mother was so
angry. Maybe it was my fault. That's why she had
always hated me.

I'd always felt more at ease with my father. He spent
time showing me things. I was fascinated by the jars of
different screws, pins, nuts and bolts he kept. He taught
me to play chess and we made models together, following diagrams from some of the books he read. He was
always reading large books on engineering. Dad could
be good fun to be with, but we never played football

together, or chase or rough and tumble. Now I knew why. He struggled to walk and he grew tired easily. He often fell asleep with a book on his knee. Mum went out a lot, shopping.

I found it difficult to settle back in England, though it was a relief not to have to follow my grandfather's rigorous regime. Everything about Western life was strange to me. I even had difficulty sleeping in a soft bed and for weeks I settled myself to sleep on the floor.

My parents enrolled me at the local comprehensive school and in the evenings I attended language classes to help with my English. I hated school. I shared nothing in common with the other boys. Their foul language and lack of respect towards the teachers came as a huge shock. In my culture of strict discipline, all elders were revered, honoured and obeyed without question.

'Hey slitty eyes, where yer going?' It was Steve Jenkins. He was leader of a gang of boys that had taunted me since my first day at the school. For weeks I had ignored them, determined to keep myself to myself. 'Off to the chinky for yer dinner, eh?' The other boys laughed as they followed me across the school yard. 'Hey Chinky, I'm talking to yer. Yer gonna ignore me then?' I carried on walking, but something was beginning to brew inside. I had let them have their fun. They didn't know what they were dealing with. One of the first principles of Kung Fu is avoid conflict, to only take action as a matter of defence. But they were not giving up. I was growing sick of their taunts and bullying. Steve Jenkins was a big, ugly lad who picked on many of the black and Asian kids. I'd seen him out with his dad. They both had shaved heads and his dad had National Front tattoos. He was a nasty piece of work.

'Come on Chinky. What's up with yer? Too scared to talk? Oh no, I forgot, you don't speak the English do yer?' With that he began dancing around in front of me, pulling his eyes into narrow slits and blocking my path. The other boys did the same, all the time laughing and egging him on. My mind went back to the day I had been beaten by the Triad children. No one would do that to me again. Jenkins came up close to my face, pulling at his eyes. 'Leave me alone,' I said, standing still and firm. Laughing he mimicked the way I spoke. 'Weave him boys, he told us to weave him awone.' He looked back at the gang for their appreciation, then turned to give me a sharp push to my left shoulder. In a flash I returned with a round house kick straight to his face, smashing his nose. He fell backwards on the ground. The other boys watched in horror as he writhed around screaming, cursing, swearing and grappling to stem the flow of blood. I looked each one straight in the eyes. They fled. It felt good.

I was mildly disciplined for the offence. The teachers knew what I had been putting up with. I was a hard-working, polite and obedient student. Steve Jenkins was a notorious bully. Not long after this incident he was expelled from school. News of my Kung Fu kick spread like wildfire among the students and I found myself with quite a posse. I wasn't used to being the centre of attention in this way. They were looking for a gang leader, for some excitement and action, but I was torn between my culture of discipline and a new, dangerously powerful, freedom. It was an intense culture shock. I didn't know how to handle myself in such a relaxed environment, where many of the teachers struggled to keep order in the classrooms. I found myself enjoying the power of an intimidating reputation. No one gave me any trouble and it was better to be a bully than to be bullied.

If not for my ongoing training, I might easily have ended up walking the same path as Steve Jenkins and his cronies.

My grandfather's reputation was such that he could secure funding for me through the International Kung Fu Federation (IKFF), based in Geneva. They arranged for me to pursue my practice at a school in Swiss Cottage, run by Mr Chang. He was a very kind, jolly man, a master of many years experience. It soon became apparent, however, that I was more advanced in many techniques. Still, I could develop under his discipline. Mr Chang encouraged me in a new way and, before long, I became an assistant instructor at the school. There, I met Kingsley who was from Jamaica and also advanced in martial arts. He became my first real friend.

The discipline of the school kept me off the streets, and out of trouble, but even Mr Chang had a very free, relaxed attitude. Somehow, it didn't fit with the harsh regime that I associated with proper training. Looking back now, I suppose I craved the firm hand that I had known for the greater part of my life. I found it, to some degree, in one of my teachers. Mr Sizer taught Religious Education. Most of the kids hated him. He was strict and stood no nonsense. I always behaved honourably towards my elders, but Mr Sizer was one of only a few teachers who I truly respected. I enjoyed RE. My grandfather had taught me much about world religions. I was fascinated by all the different practices and belief systems, but I knew that the only real god was the god within, the Ch'i. I remember Mr Sizer teaching a story from the Bible about Abraham and the way he was prepared to sacrifice his son, Isaac. What obedience to his God, Abraham demonstrated, and what bravery. It was my kind of story. Maybe I'd get hold of a Bible one day and read some more.

With the support of the IKFF, I was able to travel to martial arts competitions all over the world. Most were in Asia and my grandfather always met me there. I was aware that he gambled a great deal of money on me. I never let him down. Every year I returned to China for two or three months at a time to continue training with him. He no longer beat me, but I remained in unquestioning submission to his will.

When I was 17 he began testing me in real life combat situations. One day we travelled to Nanchang in the Jiangxi Province, south-east of the Boyang Lake. I didn't know at the time, but Nanchang is notorious for street gangs. 'Always expect the unexpected,' Lowsi told me. To my horror, he instructed me to strip down to my underwear, there and then, in the middle of the street. That was unexpected enough. I watched his face, but I should have known that it would give nothing away. He pulled a scroll out from his jacket and hung it around my neck. Sickness rose in my throat as I read the characters, 'Hum kah chan,' (Death to your family!) and 'Chao ni niang de zhu zong shi ba dai,' (Go have sex with your ancestors, grandmothers and great-grandmothers!).

Lowsi pointed me in the direction of a dark side street. 'Now walk.' I realised what he was up to. As I took a few steps forward, an old lady disappeared quickly off the street, slamming and bolting a door behind her. Suddenly, screaming obscenities filled the air and eight or nine street fighters came flying towards me with punches and kicks. The street was narrow. That was in my favour. It confined the number of opponents coming at me at one time. Quickly, I assumed a tiger stance. Using fast footwork, I concentrated on the immediate attackers. The first came at me with a right hook. I turned from my waist and blocked it with my arm, swiftly jabbing him with my right foot. As I disabled his attack the next opponent came in with a straight punch directed at my head. I turned again and deflected the punch, giving him a side kick to the face, rendering him unconscious.

Maintaining rapid footwork, I met the next opponent as he lunged at my face with his right arm. At once, I dissolved the punch in an arc, then struck him with a knuckle fist. As he plunged to the ground I used his back as a platform to move forward and gain height. The next two opponents came forward, the first with a right straight heart punch and the other with a side kick. Deflecting the quicker punch with my rising left arm block, I counter-attacked with a back fist to his temple. In the same moment I guided a backwards long-kick to the groin of the other opponent, curving my waist to dissolve his punch.

Another opponent launched himself towards me but I immediately skipped in with a flying straight thrust-kick to his temple. He fell as the next attacker came towards me with a straight fist to my chest. I swept my back in an arc and slid in with a kneeing horse, striking the opponent's groin. The final two attackers hurled glass bottles and verbal abuse at me as they ran away.

I stood for a few moments, controlling my breathing and ensuring that the fight was truly over. My grandfather appeared from nowhere and bowed to me. We made a swift exit from the scene.

We visited Nanchang and the street gangs many times over the next few years. Again and again I proved that I could handle myself in ungoverned combat. One time my grandfather made me dress up as a Chinese opera singer. He led me up a mountain to a peasant village, where he painted my face and adorned me in heavy robes. To antagonise the locals he made me shout obscenities whilst I paraded through the streets in the make-up and heavy garb. Again, I was met with multiple attackers and all manner of random weapons. My biggest challenge was being able to fight in the restrictive, thick clothing.

Not all my fights were contrived by my grandfather. Siu Ming was my cousin. Whilst travelling one day she was kidnapped and taken to work as a prostitute. This is not uncommon in China. Siu Ming was young and beautiful and, to anyone who didn't know her family name, she was an easy target. We learned that she had been taken to a brothel in Shanghai, run by Triads. There were a number of family meetings at our house and we were assured that our contacts in Shanghai would explain the misdemeanour and secure Siu Ming's immediate release. Days went by, then a letter arrived. My grandfather was angry. 'It seems our man in Shanghai is a member of the local constabulary,' he told me. 'The police are not prepared to enter Triad territory for fear of all-out street war.'

I set out for Shanghai.

My police guide would only take me so far, but it wasn't difficult to find the place. I stood outside on the street, listening to the voices inside. The door was ajar and I could hear a girl talking in a pleading manner. It might have been Siu Ming. I couldn't catch what was being said. Confidently, I stepped into the barely lit room. The girl immediately burst into tears.

'Siu Ming!' It was her. She ran and clung to me, but immediately one of the men yanked her away and pushed her into another room. I walked straight up to the desk and addressed a large, suited man who appeared to be in charge. 'I believe, sir, that there has been some mistake with that girl.'

'That girl is nothing to do with you,' he growled, barely looking up from his accounts. I was astounded that he would not even look me in the face. I spoke more firmly. 'You have kidnapped . . . '

'We have kidnapped nobody,' he interrupted.

'I don't think you understand,' I insisted, 'Siu Ming is of the Soo family in Canton. You need to release her and seek the forgiveness of my grandfather, Cheung Ling Soo.'

The man snorted in disgust. Everyone knew that to dishonour a family such as ours required the offender to seek forgiveness and pay respect. Otherwise, the families would instigate a war of killing that would span the generations. He understood what I was saying, but clearly didn't believe who I was.

'Your grandfather?' The man scoffed. 'And who are you, round eye?' he spat. Suddenly, the back door flew open and seven or eight men burst into the room brandishing their knives. I knew this could not end peacefully. I pulled out my combat cleaver and the tiger took over.

The men were left severely brutalised and I took Siu Ming home with no further opposition. That incident earned me credibility and honour among my Chinese family. It was what I had craved.

Soon afterwards, my grandfather prepared me for the challenge that would make me a 'Master' in Kung Fu. There was a series of oral and practical exams, culminating in 'Tar Shui', the 'test of the tunnel'. This test is notorious among students of Kung Fu and not many dare accept its challenge. Of the brave few who enter the tunnel, many never come out.

We travelled north for several days to the Shandong Province. The tunnel is in a cave in the base of Tai Shan, one of China's most sacred Daoist mountains. I was excited and ready for the challenge. By this point in my training I knew no fear and was eager to complete the task. It was a beautiful summer day, but as I entered the cave I could feel the chill of the mountain. After the bright sunshine, I took a moment to let my eyes adjust to the surroundings. Flaming torches partly illuminated the cavern. Several metres of broken glass lay before me. 'Easy,' I thought. Assuming the light step of the crane I barely felt a scratch as I stealthily walked over the shards. A similar test followed immediately. Hot coals. The skin on my feet was so toughened that this posed no problem. I walked confidently, not caring to rush, but eager to meet a more challenging assault. I smiled when I saw it. This was my kind of test. A wooden-framed octagonal structure blocked my path. On top of it were sharp spearheads and the whole thing was supported by only a few bamboo sticks. These were attached to a maze of horizontal and diagonal bamboo canes. I had to climb through them. Touch them, and the whole structure would collapse, bringing the spears down onto me.

I began to focus my mind. This was a test of agility and precision. Snake movements would help me steal my way through. Concentrating hard on the position of my limbs I began manoeuvring my way around, arching my back and supporting myself, when necessary, with just one hand on the floor. Using a series of flat stances and formations, I was able to ease my way between the rods until I emerged, victorious on the other side.

Next came the blade. It blocked my path and required me to walk along its razor-sharp edge. In the torchlight I could see that the floor and walls around the obstacle were shimmering. 'Oil,' I smiled. It covered the entirety of the rock. I was expected to walk the eight-metre blade to avoid the slippery surface. The cave walls were narrow at this point and there was no way around. I also sensed there was something more to this test. It would require the pinnacle of my concentration. I composed myself, harnessing the energy of the Ch'i into my feet so that I would feel no pain. Keeping perfect balance, I stepped on the blade and began to walk. Suddenly, a wild and frenzied dog came tearing down the tunnel towards me. My master had drummed into me, 'Expect the unexpected.' Immediately, I recognised the dog as a distraction trap. Sure enough, in its madness it tried to lunge at me, but it was held back by a heavy chain. My control of the Ch'i ensured perfect calm. I continued to walk the blade.

Bypassing the wild dog, I moved further through the cave, my senses heightened. The tunnel began to widen again. Then I saw it. The width of the cave was blocked by a wooden platform. It had trident spearheads sticking out from its facing edge and it was mounted on a large boulder. The whole structure stood on large metal-rimmed wooden wheels that looked as though they had never been moved. This was, by far, the biggest challenge yet. There was no clear surface area to push against, only that covered by the spears.

I slipped into my meditation so that I could move the energy of the Ch'i into my hands. Boldly, I pushed my palms onto the points. I summoned maximum force, but the structure did not budge. Raising one foot up onto a spike I tried again. Still nothing. I would not be beaten. I rested, still meditating and concentrating on harnessing the Ch'i. I would try another tactic. Turning around, I placed my back against the spears, hoping that the larger surface area would give extra force.

For years I had practised this kind of spear stress tolerance with my grandfather. As a regular exercise he would lean his full weight behind a spear as he pushed into my torso. Like a dry sponge, the flesh and muscle is weak and easily penetrated. But when the sponge is soaked in water it becomes tough and strong. Similarly, when all the energy of the body is concentrated into one place, such as the abdomen, the skin and muscles can become as solid as rock. I rarely sustained any injury, other than the slight scratching of the surface skin.

The structure creaked under the pressure. Encouraged, I continued to push, but I was beginning to feel the spears cutting into my back. Returning to my original flat palm position, I refocused my energy and, closing my eyes, I began mentally moving the structure inmind. My hands took the strain and my whole being was concentrated on moving the object. It budged, but the wheels refused to turn. Again, I set my mind and called on the power of my breathing. I would not let Lowsi down. I would make him proud. With a final assault I forced the structure about half a metre down the cave, falling to my knees as the energy rushed through my body and into the rock. I afforded myself a satisfied smile before squeezing through the tiny space I had opened.

Stepping ever cautiously, I realised the cave was growing lighter. My test was almost over but I knew, by its legacy, the obstacle that lay ahead. Sure enough, I began to smell burning iron. Soon I could see the opening of the cave and my grandfather silhouetted in the sunlight. Blocking my exit was a large cauldron of burning iron filings. It was glowing red with the heat and looked like it weighed several hundred pounds. Metal tiger claws stuck out from the sides and I could see the dragon emblems, waiting to take my flesh. This was the final test of bravery, strength and endurance. I focused momentarily on Lowsi's face. As usual, it was blank. I didn't need the encouragement of any facial gesture. His presence alone was enough.

I calmed myself and summoned the Ch'i into my arms. In a few moments they grew icy cold and numb. Setting my eyes straight ahead I placed my forearms on the burning hot dragons. There was the instant smell of burning hair and flesh, but it meant nothing. I felt nothing. Using the strength of my tiger limbs, I forced the energy upwards through my lower body and lifted the mighty urn. Avoiding any more damage to myself, I held it away from my body, at a distance from the protruding tiger claws. In a controlled stagger, I heaved it out of the cave and set it before my master. His face broke, just enough to honour me with a small smile. I pulled my arms away from the burning cauldron. They were still icy cold from my meditation, but looking down I could see hot blisters beginning to form where the dragons had burned into my forearms.

Lowsi gave me the sign of fealty. (This is the sign of respect and honour used between opponents, and between student and master. It represents the Ch'i, the yin and yang, sun and moon. The right hand is made into a fist, representing the moon, and the left hand is open, representing the sun, with its heel laying flat on the fist.) Before any exercise or combat, I devoted myself to my master using this sign. Now he gave it back to me. It was my highest honour. He presented me with an ornate sword. It signified my new status. I was now Lo Fu Zai, Master in the way of Kung Fu.

Chapter 5

As a Master in the art of my ancestors, I was fully committed to preserving the legacy of the Soo family name. My grandfather's teachings and his personal honour were at stake every time I entered the arena. It was a burden I accepted with great pride.

Some of my finest moments were at the Ashraf Tae School in Karachi, Pakistan. Ashraf and my grandfather had met as young Shaolin warriors in northern China. Both had gone on to become renowned Grand Masters. Ashraf studied and developed various fighting techniques, including 'Monkey Warrior', 'Coiling Serpent' and the dragon system of southern China. Whilst both men had deep respect for one another's mastery in the way of Kung Fu, there had always been intense rivalry between them. Both had opposing ideas when it came to passing on and preserving their art. Until my arrival, my grandfather had never found a suitable disciple to whom he would fully disclose his secrets. Ashraf, on the other hand, had freely recruited hundreds of young boys, many of them from local peasant families, who he trained in the way of Kung Fu. His school was renowned in martial arts circles, but Lowsi remained cynical and scathing about his students' motives and commitment. 'They fight with anger and human strength,' he scoffed. 'They display little authentic artistic accuracy in their moves.'

Ashraf, however, was triumphant in his reputation and apparent success. For years, Lowsi had waited quietly in the wings. Now it was time. Through me, he expected to tip the balance and prove his techniques and teachings as far superior. I had much to prove.

One of Grand Master Ashraf's most acclaimed students was Raani. His core training was in 'Monkey Warrior' techniques. 'Ashraf believes you are equally matched,' Lowsi told me as we travelled to Pakistan. When I saw Raani I noticed that we shared the same thin, muscular stature, although he was slightly taller. As both our masters had predicted, we met in the final of a knockout tournament that had involved some fifteen fighters.

I was first into the circle. There was a subdued ripple of applause, then a hushed anticipation fell among the crowd. Lowsi was seated with Ashraf at the side of the ring, with his eyes fixed on me. I waited. Suddenly, the crowd erupted, shouting, cheering and clapping as their hero, Raani, took his place in front of me. We showed fealty to one another. He wore farmer's clothes and looked rough and unkempt, but the crowd loved him. He was their man. They continued to chant his name and shout wishes of good luck. No one shouted for me. I stared at my master. He looked calm and confident. That was the reassurance I needed.

The judge was a diminutive man named Denju. Raising his arms to hush the expectant crowd, he instructed Raani and I to prepare. The crowd fell silent, though many continued to motion their bets. A moment later, Denju clapped his hands and all attention was locked in the ring.

Assuming a fighting tiger stance, I raised my hands to a guard position, with flattened tiger claws. I planned to combine my favourite tiger moves with the leopard system, which is three times faster than the tiger, but not as strong. Our eyes bore into each other as I began to inch towards Raani. He assumed a very low, slightly twisted fighting horse. Waiting for my advance, he squared his shoulders toward me and dropped his weight to his rear leg. I concentrated on anticipating his moves and couldn't help noticing the inaccuracy of his position. Such a slovenly technique would have incurred a severe beating from Lowsi. He shuffled back and forth, whilst weaving and bobbing, sometimes touching the ground with one or both of his fists.

We closed distance cautiously, keeping our eyes locked on one another. The crowd remained silent as Raani began to circle, trying to deceive me. He feigned a movement to his left. Just as I began to adjust my stance to meet it, he rolled towards my legs. In a flash, I jumped over his monkey roll attack. Raani grasped at my left leg. In a powerful hamstring response I delivered a sharp heel hook to the monkey's arm. We both came crashing to the floor as the crowd heaved in anticipation. Leaping up, I assumed a leopard stance and attacked the rising monkey with a series of speedy kicks.

Raani blocked well, backing away quickly from the rushing leopard. He reached toward the edge of the circle. For a moment I was confused. Would he give up this easily? He appeared to be stepping out of the ring, when suddenly he flew at me. Instantly, I hit out with a stab kick to the groin. He'd anticipated my move and took the blow so that he could grab my right sleeve. His deception was perfect, but I immediately saw the danger. I had taken too many beatings from my master not to recognise it. Time after time he had delivered this basic throw and I had suffered the painful consequences.

The monkey instantly slipped beneath my leopard barrage and pulled down on my sleeve, while thrusting a kick up into my groin. I rose into the air, pain sweeping through me like a lightning bolt.

In a split second I regained my focus and diverted the pain, twisting to land on my feet. There were gasps in the crowd as I fought to control my balance. I had one foot in the ring and the other on the wooden circle. The monkey flew at me again, trying to knock me out of the ring. I ran a few steps down the curved beam. Now the deception was mine. I balanced for a moment, then both of my hands went to my groin as I bent over and started to collapse from the agony. The pain was genuine enough, but as the monkey quickly turned, running to push me again, I spun on the beam, swept the monkey's hands down and leopard punched him hard in the side of the neck. Raani's eyes rolled back and he collapsed to the ground.

For a moment, the arena was silent. Denju counted, 'One, two, three, out,' and pointed to me as the winner. The crowd erupted in a deafening roar of applause. I had earned their respect and honour. Raani came back to consciousness and sat groggily, accepting my sign of fealty, but hardly meeting my gaze. I turned towards Lowsi and the other elders, also giving them the sign of respect. My master stood in applause. It was my greatest honour.

A few months later another tournament was set. Once again, Lowsi and I travelled to Pakistan where I had been invited to fight Raani's uncle, Adnan. It was an unfair matching and I was concerned that this is where my reputation would fall. Might this even be one of Lowsi's strategies to teach me a lesson? Perhaps he didn't expect me to win at all. Adnan was a Master in the Mountain Crane system and several years ahead of me in training. 'This will not be a public fight,' Lowsi informed me. Closed door fights always meant there was a lot of money at stake.

Adnan shared the same peasant look as his nephew. As our eyes locked, his weather-beaten face was determined, focused and mean. The honour of his Master was at stake and he meant business.

As the tiger, I would try to get close to Adnan using aggression, strength and power. I knew the crane's way would be to avoid direct confrontation. He would dodge and weave or slip away then make his strike from a distance. There was much new ground for me. I had studied a mixed tiger and crane system, but I had never seen fighters from these two opposing animal systems in combat against each other.

Sure enough, as I aggressively pursued Adnan, he seemed to ride the air, easily avoiding my tiger punches, kicks and sweeping claws. My strikes were far more powerful than his, but I could not seem to hit my target. Realising my misjudgement, I began to inwardly question my strategy. As if sensing this wave of insecurity, Adnan took his chance. He swung gracefully over my hard sweeping back fist blow, and used crane feathers to lightly rake across my eyes. Blinded, I lost my guard.

The tall skinny crane took full advantage. Dropping his hands to the ground, he swept his leg in a hard fast arc through my legs. My feet flew up as high as his chest before the weight of his body came down on me. My upper back and shoulders came crashing to the ground. As my eyes began to focus, I caught sight of Lowsi leaping up from his seat at the side of the ring. I would not let him be dishonoured this way.

Springing up, I raised my guard, but the crane attacked again, before I could even regain my breath. Adnan landed several hard whirling crane fists to my head. I wrestled to regain focus as he moved in to strike my body. The head shots were dizzying, but now, new determination fired through my veins. As Adnan drew closer I suddenly grasped his tiring left forearm with my right hand and squeezed. He had not anticipated the move. Adnan screeched in pain and lashed out with a front snap kick. I dug into a nearly flat horse stance and pulled the crane's arm to the side, throwing his incoming kick off target. Squeezing harder and harder I set about forcing the crane to the ground. With a full-throated cry he fell to his knees and struggled with the pain until he could bear no more. 'I yield! I yield,' he screamed.

When I later met my grandfather, he had a twinkle in his eye, which I had not seen before. He patted the pocket of his gown. I learned that my victory had secured him the equivalent of a year's earnings. I should have known he would never have done himself the dishonour of gambling against me.

Back in England, I continued to work at Mr Chang's school. My father became increasingly frail and relied on me to lift him and get him around. Mother still went out a lot. Living with them, I began to understand something of their relationship. They were an odd couple. Both were born in England, yet raised in the strong traditions of their respective Italian and Chinese cultures. Their families strongly disapproved of their union and they were ostracised by both sides. They were cultural misfits. My mother remained proud of her ancestry, but she had a superior demeanour that endeared her to few. She had a taste for the finer things in life, but when illness meant my father could no longer work, my mother's aspirations to the affluent lifestyle were shattered. She kept up a certain pretence, dressing up to visit the fine stores of Knightsbridge and Regent Street. Always she returned home to a council house and a benefit book.

As the months went by, Mr Chang rewarded me with a wage increase as I took on more teaching at the school.

I gave all my earnings to my parents. In the meantime, the IKFF was taking care of my travel expenses for competitions. I remained undefeated and they soon began to show interest in my future career. I was encouraged to enter the World Championships. At first this had little appeal. Many of the Grand Masters of Kung Fu refused to recognise the championships. Such a title is of little consequence to the way of Kung Fu. Masters entered their students into competitions purely to help them develop combat technique. International acclaim and adulation is never an incentive.

'It just seems so arrogant to me,' I said to my friend, Kingsley, as we walked home from Mr Chang's school. 'I only fight to honour my master.'

'Yes, but it's an easy one for you. Come on, Tony, the World Championship, that's an honour worth having, eh?' He dug me in the ribs, laughing, 'And man, what couldn't you do with £10,000 prize money!' Kingsley could always make me smile. Perhaps he was right. I would discuss it with Lowsi.

I entered the World Championships for three years running, once in Thailand and twice in Hong Kong. The tournaments are always 'point' rather than 'full contact' competitions. That way, no one gets seriously hurt, and fighters have to demonstrate control and fine technique. Each year I found myself among four accomplished fighters in the final heats. I relished the challenge. Li Chang Po from Xi'an was my biggest opponent. He was a student of the renowned Grand Master, Gwok Siu Fong. We had met several times over the years, at various temple demonstrations, and there was a deep respect between us. Any rivalry was abandoned in mutual regard. We both recognised we had endured similar training and fought with the same motivation. Our fights were tough, but I beat him for two years running. In my third year as a competitor, I was disappointed to find that Li Chang Po had not entered. I took the title with great ease that year.

The prize money went straight to my grandfather. He then sent a decent share back to me and I gave a substantial sum to my parents.

During this time I was invited to work directly for the IKFF. I began travelling to many places around the world, monitoring schools of Kung Fu and registering teachers. Preserving the way of Kung Fu is the fundamental concern of the IKFF. Funding for the organisation comes from a close protection service that they offer to governments, organisations and individuals who require personal security. It wasn't long before I was invited to join the staff, training recruits in hand-to-hand combat. The perks were good. They paid me good money, provided a motorbike and set me up in a flat, close to the main training warehouse, on the Rue de La Confederation in Geneva, Switzerland. Most of the students were ex-military and I met men from all nationalities and walks of life. They were all tough guys, many from the French Foreign Legion, the British Army special forces or the American military. They all had basic training in combat and weaponry, but the job of the IKFF was to advance their skills in all areas of defence and protection. Ultimately these men were responsible for the safety of the world's elite, the most rich and powerful.

Most of the guys felt quite at home in weapons training, but my mission was to demonstrate that hand-to-hand combat could be equally efficient in a threatening situation. Over a number of weeks I took them through basic full contact moves and blocks. Using live action tests they played out their skills in hostage situations, pursuits, escapes and all manner of close quarter and wide range combat scenarios.

There was a great camaraderie between us. They were tough guys who liked to party. When we weren't working we would hit the local clubs and bars. Many of them took drugs and drank heavily but such vices never had any appeal to me. I was still doing five or six hours a day personal training. I needed a clear head to remain at the peak of my discipline. Still, there was much that I liked about the bodyguard lifestyle. It was exciting, with a sense of danger that had great appeal. They met and mixed with some of the wealthiest people in the world and had many of their client's luxurious facilities at their disposal.

Jean Lomme was becoming a good friend. He was a Canadian – a tall guy with a broad smile, thick curly hair and a wicked sense of humour. He had trained in the French Foreign Legion and had already worked for some years in close protection units. One night we were out to dinner with Sasha, who was from Belgium, and Mohammed from India. I sat back and listened to their conversation. They were swapping stories about their employers. 'Man, that was a good one,' boasted Jean. 'Three months on the beach in Mauritius. What more could a man ask for? Great house by the ocean, the yacht and my choice of a Jag or BMW 7 series. Nice work!'

'You call that working? C'mon man, what about the action?' Mohammed goaded. 'Lying around on board a yacht, it'd bore me stupid,' he scoffed.

Jean feigned offence. 'It had its moments. This man had serious business . . . '

'Yeah, yeah, I bet the most action you got was diving off the boat for a swim!'

'Like I could swim with a gun down my trunks?' Jean came back, pretending to pull his weapon out and hold it across the table at Mohammed's head. Mohammed laughed out loud.

'C'mon then man, anytime, anytime,' he said, patting his jacket pocket at his chest. Most of the bodyguards carried guns at all times.

'Hey Tony, what's wrong with you, man?' said Sasha, with a wink at the others. 'You wanna stop playing around with the teaching and get where the action is.'

'He's right,' Mohammed joined in. 'You're wasted with all this. And think of all those lonely rich ladies, just waiting for a little protection from a nice boy like you.' They all laughed.

'Yeah, I really wanna be some kind of fashion accessory like you guys,' I retorted with a grin. The conversation degenerated into stories of rich women who sported their bodyguards like their diamond earrings, or fur coats. But it wasn't all like that. I knew that these men might well be involved in highly dangerous world-scale security issues. They were the elite, trained to handle themselves in any kind of terrorist attack, taking full responsibility for the defence of world leaders, diplomats, royalty and high-ranking government officials. Yes, I could fancy a bit of that.

The IKFF welcomed my decision and sent me on all the courses to qualify me as a bodyguard. There was much to learn. I had little experience of firearms, but I turned out to be a decent shot and soon got to grips with how to handle and maintain the various weapons. Through real life case studies and battle scenarios we were trained in the use of telescopic-lensed rifles (for counter-sniper operations), high velocity semi-automatic carbines (to engage targets at distance), pump action twelve gauge shotguns and a variety of handguns, pistols and revolvers. Still, I was most comfortable with hand-to-hand combat. A knife, rather than a gun, would always be my choice. I shared much in common with the instructor who coached us in the use of knives and similar weaponry. He was Burmese and had undergone a similar training to me. The Tiger system of Kung Fu originated in Burma and he often had me demonstrate tiger blocks and attacks using a knife or machete.

I attended courses in protective driving, surveillance, alarms, para-medicine, international criminal law, anti-terrorism, communications and explosives, among many others. There was a great deal of study, with endless written assignments and we were all tutored in the basics of the world's main languages. I rose to the challenge and was graded highly in all areas. Before long I was able to take the bodyguard's oath. Our slogan was 'Deum Solem Timidus' ('In God alone we fear'). It made me smile. I feared no God. There was no God, only the god within.

My first on-the-job training assignment was with Winston. He was an experienced Chicago born body-guard who had worked for the same client for a number of years. Diane was an extremely wealthy Dutch lady, living in Switzerland. I was amazed when I first arrived at her huge, secluded residence in the mountains. I had never seen such affluence. Apart from occasional shopping trips and visits to art galleries, Diane lived an isolated life with her young son, Gregory, and a handful of domestic staff. Gregory was a precocious child, but working with Winston was good. There was much I could learn from him about security procedure, surveillance and close protection when out with the 'principals'. I gathered the main threat was from Diane's estranged husband. She had won legal custody of Gregory, but her husband was a renowned gangster. It was feared that he might try to snatch the child at some point. During the time Winston had been working with them there had been no such action. The IKFF considered Diane and her son to be relatively low risk, ideal for a training assignment. I looked forward to the day I would work with a fully-manned five-unit surveillance and close protection team. The principal in such cases was at highest risk, usually a prime target for assassination.

After a while, Winston was taken off the case to work on another project and I was left alone. One day I got a message on the radio from the security guard who patrolled the grounds near the gate. 'Just letting you know, Tony, there's a delivery coming through.'

'Delivery? What delivery?'

'Oh, I don't know. It's just a white van, laundry or something. Two guys up front in white overalls, you know the type.'

'No. Find out who they are and what they are delivering.' I quickly checked the schedule for the week, knowing that nothing was due that day. 'Oh, sorry Tony, I've already let them in.'

'Idiot. What are you thinking of?' I was livid. Diane was out and Gregory was on the second floor of the house with his au pair. I burst in on them. 'Stay where you are and don't come out of this room,' I yelled at the young girl's startled face. Flying down the huge staircase I forgot all my training and protocol. I should have remained with the boy and called the police immediately, but no, my mind was on the intruders.

I opened the front door to a shotgun, pushed straight in my face. 'We've come for the boy,' demanded the man behind the gun in French. I couldn't see beyond the door frame and had no idea how many men there were. The security guard had told me there was only one van, with two people up front. I glared at the gunman and could tell that another stood just behind him, off to the left side. There was a good chance that others had been hiding in the back of the van. I had to think quickly.

Walking forward into the gun allowed me to clear the door frame. I knew he would not shoot that quickly and it gave me a split second to ascertain how many intruders I was actually dealing with. Another three were standing to the right-hand side. As far as I could tell in that moment, they were unarmed, but I caught sight of a revolver in the hand of the second man. In a flash, I hit the shotgun away from me and turned it around, into the face of the gunman. As the second raised his weapon I did a high kick, knocking the revolver flying over the heads of the other three and sending him crashing to the ground. That was a bad move. Now any of them who could get enough distance would get to the gun and I would be dead. I rammed the double barrel into the face of the first man and flew over to the other three, punching and kicking like a wild man. They fell in turn. Pulling myself off them I could see the second guy stumbling over, just about reaching the gun. Stepping on one of the fallen men to gain height, I leapt onto his back, delivering a long-snap tiger fist into the back of his head. He fell, momentarily unconscious, whilst the others writhed in agony.

The security guard, by this time, had suspected something was wrong and had radioed through to the kitchen. The cook phoned for the police. By the time they arrived I had lined up the groaning and injured men on the steps of the house. I stood guard over them with the shotgun.

I could not be proud of myself. I had left my charge and broken the first fundamental rule of close protection. I was still only very young, much too full of my own abilities and eager for a fight. Had it gone wrong I would have put Gregory and the staff in serious danger. It was a hard lesson, but I would not have to learn it again.

Over the next few years I rose through the ranks in close protection security. Some of my clients were under serious threat of abduction, revenge attack or murder. I proved myself in hair-raising situations and, as one of the IKFF's senior bodyguards, I was at the special request of some of the world's most powerful people.

For several months I worked with an American, William Black. He was a savvy businessman, with serious investment in many of the prominent buildings in midtown Manhattan. I became his principal bodyguard. He liked to refer to me as his 'point man'. Apparently, it had a lot to do with my habit of jabbing my finger towards people whilst talking to them.

It was my business to know everything about him, from his business affairs to the type of bread he wanted for his lunchtime sandwich. Then there were the women. William was a serial womaniser of grand proportion. To my annoyance his 'affairs' often impacted his daily schedule and I found myself having to adapt our itinerary throughout the day. That kind of thing just created extra work and pressure for me and the rest of the team. Depending on where he was travelling, and the nature of his business, his protection varied from just me and one other guy, to a five man team, over which I had command.

Theoretically, he was safe whilst in the United States. The minute he stepped foot on a plane, however, he became more at risk. For a rich, powerful and high profile businessman, international travel massively upped the stakes, especially when we were in a country of anti-US sentiment.

One day a report came through from William's PA. His people had arranged a meeting for him in Saudi Arabia. I read the brief and slammed it down on my desk. 'Trouble?' asked Henry, my colleague. 'We're off to

Saudi. Only a week to prepare,' I said angrily. 'These people have no idea do they?'

I worked late that night, preparing a risk assessment.

William was to meet with the Fahali brothers, two notorious, politically influential investors, in Riyadh. The brothers were unhappy that one of their businesses had been acquired in a hostile takeover by William's organisation several months earlier. They had requested this meeting to negotiate with him directly regarding the return of the family concern. My boss stood to gain even more profit through a deal with them, but the problem was that the original business had already been broken up for resale. It had reached a point of no return. There were issues to negotiate, but in many ways, William's hands were tied.

Business involving such heated family interest seriously increased the risk to my client. I knew this assignment could be dangerous, especially in that part of the world. As far as I was concerned, we would be walking into unpredictable, hostile territory. My report highlighted that this proposition carried too many risks to my client. His safety was my number one priority. I recommended that the meeting, if it needed to involve William personally, should be rearranged to take place on more neutral territory. At the very least, if we were to go ahead with the journey to Saudi Arabia, my team needed more time to make necessary checks and arrangements.

I received a faxed reply within the day. They had put my report to William's legal office but it had been discounted. 'Mr Black's advisors suggest that the financial leverage of this engagement outweighs the possibility of any risk,' it read. 'Therefore, since we do not expect to jeopardise the IKFF's contract with Mr Black in any way, we request that you make speedy preparations to accompany your client to Saudi Arabia.'

In annoyance, I scribbled a fax to Sandra Zaple in Switzerland. She was always my point of contact at head office for all overseas travel and surveillance operations. Next, I grabbed the phone and summoned Henry to report to me as soon as he could.

'Hello my darlings,' came Sandra's voice over the speakerphone. Henry and I smirked at each other. Neither of us had met Sandra in person, but she was always very bubbly and familiar on the phone and there was a lot of harmless flirtation between us. 'Good afternoon Sandra,' I said. 'A fine mess we've got to deal with this time,' I joked.

'Yes, my darling, but we just do as we're told don't we? What can we say if our clients insist on such craziness?'

'We've got a lot of work to do,' I said, focusing the conversation. 'Black's people won't allow us to take the full team, so just Henry and I will travel with him and his two colleagues to Riyadh.'

'They've no idea what they might be walking into have they?' said Henry with disdain. 'Still, I suppose we'll move quicker if things get heated when there's just the two of us.' Henry was a good friend and colleague. He was British, of Nepalese descent and had done his basic training with the Gurkhas. He was taller and of much bigger build than me, with a lot of experience under his belt. There were very few people I trusted, and Henry was one of them.

We went through the details of the job with Sandra, sharing the preparation work between us. 'Our RSO (Regional Security Officer) is a chap named Abdullah Alkaff,' reported Sandra. 'I'll put a photograph in the mail to you, but he's a master of disguise. Most of the time he looks like one of the peasants, but this guy can get you anything from Dim Sum to a guided missile.'

'Hmmm, Dim Sum in Saudi, that I've got to try,' I said.

'Abdullah will arrange local drivers and on-the-ground communications, which he'll channel through me,' Sandra continued. 'I'll have an exact itinerary, ordinance survey and building maps to you by this time tomorrow.'

Our visit was planned to last no more than three days from the time we arrived in Saudi Arabia. The flight was exhausting: over twelve hours, with refuelling stops in the UK and Bahrain. The days leading up to the trip had required round the clock preparation, so both Henry and I were thankful to schedule in some sleep time in the air.

As we landed in Riyadh, my heart began to beat faster and adrenaline pumped through my body. Perhaps I was just being over cautious. Certainly tiredness was making me edgy, but I had an uncomfortable feeling about this assignment.

Chapter 6

Abdullah had arranged for William's private jet to park in the Presidential slot at Riyadh airport. There'd be two white Mercedes to meet us, but we still had to clear the main terminal building. It was mobbed with people and we were way too exposed for my liking. I walked in front, scanning the crowd for any hint of potential threat. Henry took up the rear, keeping his eyes fixed on William and his two sidekicks. They were casual, chatting and laughing as we moved through the crowd. They could easily get in the way or slow us down in an emergency. People pushed and shoved and bag handlers jostled and fought for business. I was tense. My senses were on overdrive, ready to react quickly. This wasn't a situation I could control and I didn't like it.

'Baksheesh, baksheesh,' nagged a ferret-faced man as he tried to force our bags from my hand. I shoved him hard. 'Easy, point man, easy,' laughed William. 'Not so heavy-handed. It's just their way.' I knew that. In the last week I'd been reading all I could about Arabic culture. 'Baksheesh' was a culturally-expected tip, a system through which people with means are expected to share their money with the less wealthy. Fine, but right now I had other things on my mind. I wouldn't be happy until we were clear of the place.

Henry and I climbed into the first Mercedes with William. We would never leave his side. The two colleagues followed in the second car. Still, I couldn't fully relax. The IKFF had local contacts in just about every country of the world, but it wasn't my nature to trust anyone. I preferred to use my own network when possible. Despite Sandra's assurances, I'd never met this Abdullah and was instinctively cautious about him and his people. With unknown drivers, I was immediately on my guard.

Le Meridian hotel was dripping in gold ornamentation and decked in marble from top to bottom. William was assigned a luxurious top floor penthouse suite. I entered first and did a basic security check, checking for IEDs (Improvised Explosive Devices). When I was satisfied, my client settled himself for the evening. Henry was on shift that night. I welcomed the sleep.

The next morning I rose early to carry out security checks before William got up. It was the day of the meeting. I covered the whole of the floor, lifts, stairs, lobby, restaurant and kitchens, finishing with the two cars. I fully expected a sophisticated range of ESDs (Electronic Surveillance Devices), but I found nothing. William was still tired and sluggish when I met him. The previous day's flight had been draining. He was a short man with thinning fair hair and a little too much weight for his stature. Still, he had a notable presence about him, the kind of self-assurance that wealth and power bring.

Before we left for the meeting I ran through the day's protocol with Henry and William. 'Whatever happens, do not move from my sight,' I warned William. We agreed that I would be introduced as his personal advisor, giving Henry the appearance of firsthand bodyguard. Henry did a second security check on the cars and we were away.

The Fahali brothers' building was even more ornate than Le Meridian. Their welcome was warm and friendly. As introductions were taking place I assimilated the area in my mind, mentally checking the exits and

staircases. I had studied the plans of the building that
Sandra had sent to us. I knew the air conditioning chan-
nels and all vent shafts that might be used as an escape
route in an emergency.

'This is a safe building,' said one of the brothers to
William as he eyed Henry. 'Why don't you let your
bodyguard rest in the lounge?' As rehearsed, I gave
Henry the nod, releasing him from our guard. It was
easy for the brothers to believe Henry as the firsthand
man. He looked much tougher than me. I knew he
would make good use of his time.

The men chatted a while over drinks and baklava (a
rich, flaky pastry), then the meeting began in earnest. It
started very calmly. One of William's colleagues began
explaining the difficulty of the disintegration and resale
of parts of the business. He hadn't been talking for long
when Fahali voices were raised in anger. One brother
appeared to quickly lose his temper. 'My family has not
invested time and money in this business to see it ripped
to shreds by you yanks.'

'Now slowly,' warned his brother, keeping much
calmer. I had a feeling they were playing good cop bad
cop with us.

'No,' interrupted the more heated brother, slamming
his hand down on the table. 'Someone must pay for this
assault on our name.'

As the meeting grew more heated I watched the brothers like a hawk, sensing that the situation was rapidly
degenerating. I trusted that Henry would be in place.
William took over the dialogue, but the brothers rejected
his attempts at negotiation. Suddenly the aggressive
brother stood up. My hand instinctively went to my
inside pocket. He spoke to his brother in Arabic, then
stormed out of the room. There was a moment's silence
before the other brother spoke of his disgust. 'We will be

taking measures to secure our interests,' he spat. I took the lead and guided William quickly out of the room.

I was relieved to see Henry standing by the car. Things didn't look good though. He was surrounded by six burly-looking men in dark glasses and western suits. Henry read my face. As we approached the cars a man I had not seen before stepped out from behind us and shouted to the men in Arabic. They started to move towards us. I would happily have taken them on, taught them all a good lesson, but William's safety was of paramount importance. I had to stick close to him. The men did nothing, except guide us to our car. I can only assume they had been instructed to ensure we left the building.

As we settled ourselves in the Mercedes, sweat began pouring off William. 'Phew, that was not pleasant,' he said.

'It's not over yet,' I replied, noting that the heavies had split. One group got into a black BMW and sped off at high speed in front of us. The others were piling into another car. 'Drive!' I instructed our man. Omar, another peasant-like man, sat in the front seat next to the driver. He had been sourced by Abdullah to accompany us as a translator. Again, I was instinctively wary of him. I sat close to William in the back of the car. Henry wrestled the box of firearms, stored in the boot, through the back seat.

As we drove off, I noticed in the rear view mirror that the second BMW was following our convoy. 'We've got problems,' I said. Henry and I could communicate a lot to each other just with a look. He knew I did not trust the men in the front of our car. I kept my eyes fixed on them and he took up the rear view.

'Shit!' he exclaimed. I shot a look behind. The heavies in the second BMW had overtaken our following car and were directly behind us. I was furious. This would never have happened if we'd used our own drivers. Our men were trained to drive in high-speed convoys with less than a foot between the cars. They would never have allowed the two Mercedes to become separated in this way. I grabbed a gun and shoved it in the back of our driver's head. He wailed and began crying out to Allah.

As I feared, the intervening car slowed down, forcing the second Mercedes with William's colleagues to stop. Two men got out. They walked back to the Mercedes and, with handguns, fired shots through the rear side windows.

I leapt on top of William, forcing him down behind the front seats. 'Go!' I yelled at the whimpering driver. He put his foot down, but we'd not gone far before he came to an emergency stop. I sprang up and pushed my gun to his head, yelling at him to keep driving. Instead, he leapt out of the car and began scrambling away, screaming for his life. I still didn't know whether he was in on the operation. Had he driven us into an ambush, or was he truly terrified and breaking with the pressure? We didn't have time to find out.

Henry leapt over the front seat and took the wheel. We stood more chance now. Henry was one of the IKFF's most accomplished drivers. Sure enough, we sped through the dusty streets at high speed. They became narrow and crowded with people, stalls and animals and we had no idea even what direction we were heading in. The BMW was in hot pursuit and Henry lost none of his momentum, expertly manoeuvring the car as people scattered in our wake. At high speed, we weaved through idling traffic, kicking up dust clouds and hitting the odd vehicle in our haste to lose the mob. 'Whoa!' yelled Henry as we crashed straight through the middle of a stall. A startled Arab leapt out of the way, just in time, as dates and figs came raining down on the car. The fabric roof of the stall was carried along on the windscreen and Henry blindly drove flat out until it fell to the side of the road.

Keeping William's head buried I poked my gun at Omar who was desperately trying to work out where we were. He clearly had no idea. 'Get us to the embassy,' I yelled, 'British or American. Come on man, think!'

'Here, here, take left,' he said, fearing for his life.

Henry spun the car down a narrow street. 'No, no, not it,' cried the increasingly frenzied translator. 'Try here.'

Henry switched right onto a wider main street. 'Road block!' he suddenly cried.

I shoved the gun harder at the man's head. Had he led us into this? Henry spun the car through ninety degrees and took a street that lead into a narrow, dark, alleyway. 'Hold on!' Our wing mirrors clipped the side of the buildings, but Henry didn't slow down. We broke out into daylight. Another crowded street. Omar, by this time, was sobbing with fear. I stole a glance behind. We seemed to have lost the BMW.

'Stop the car,' I instructed Henry. He pulled up sharp. 'Get out! Get out!' I yelled at the translator. Omar grappled to open the door. Cursing, swearing and fearing for his life, he fell from the car as Henry put his foot down again.

Finally we hit lucky, breaking out from the labyrinth of the town, onto more open road. All we could see ahead was desert. We drove on for a couple of hours. 'We've got to ditch the car,' said Henry. 'They'll be looking for us.' We carried on in silence. I racked my brains, trying to formulate a plan. We had to get William out of the country by undercover means. There was a safe site in Jordan, with good people I knew I could trust, but we were probably at least 800 kilometres away. I'd totally lost trust in Abdullah, so all our Saudi contacts were void. There were other safe houses in Kuwait and Bahrain. Bahrain must be the nearest. If we could contact Sandra, she could arrange the paperwork there to get us overseas. Henry interrupted my thoughts, 'The fuel light's been on for the last few miles.'

'You're kidding?'

'Nope. The car couldn't have been full when we started.'

I shook my head in disgust. It was the first rule of protective driving: always have a full tank. I looked at William. He was seated upright by now, but was shaking, sweating and bright red in the face. I wondered how far he'd make it on foot. We had no idea where we were heading or how far it was to the next town. It was September and still stinking hot in the desert. I checked our emergency supplies. There was a little food and four small bottles of mineral water. It wouldn't get us far, especially in the heat.

The decision was soon taken out of my hands. 'OK, that's it,' said Henry, slamming his hands on the driving wheel as the car ground to a halt. 'Out of gas.' William sat on the side of the road, loosening his tie and holding his hanky on his head to shield himself from the sun. Henry and I pushed the car off the road into some vegetation. It was impossible to completely conceal it.

We set off, walking. We hadn't come across any traffic, but I was anxious to get off the highway. 'I reckon it might lead to Harad,' said Henry. To our left, the land was barren and scrub-like. To the right was a vast expanse of desert. 'If we keep going parallel with the road we should make it by nightfall.'

'How sure are you?'

'Not at all.'

I had no ideas of my own and trusted Henry's instinct. I yanked a water bottle away from William. He was glugging it down, letting it drip from his chin, onto his chest. 'We've got to be disciplined with the water,' I told him. 'We don't know how long we're going to be out here.'

After a few hours walking we found some shade among larger rocks on the scrubland and rested a while. 'Reckon we've only got a couple more hours of daylight,' said Henry. I'd feel safer in the dark, but the desert could be freezing cold at night. With each passing moment I was growing more anxious.

Finally, we reached a town. 'Well done,' I said to Henry, slapping him on the back. It was Harad. By then it was dark and William was shivering with the extreme changes in temperature. The streets were quiet. There were a few groups of men, standing together smoking and chatting, but they moved off quickly when they saw us approaching. 'Thanks for your help,' said William sarcastically. Eventually we came across a building that might have been a petrol station. A weather-beaten Arab viewed us through narrow eyes as we walked in. Henry and William started gathering food and drinks. 'I need to use your telephone,' I said, part in English, part in poor Arabic, part gesture. The man stared at me and did nothing. I was sure he'd understood. William came up and opened his wallet. The man looked lustfully at the wad of notes and smiled. He picked the phone from behind the counter and handed it to me.

It was a relief to hear Sandra's voice. Knowing how vulnerable we were in that place, I quickly filled her in on our situation. 'You're about 100 kilometres from the safe house in Bahrain,' she told me. 'Head east. I'll get passports sorted so you can get out.' She gave me coded details of a place and contact, just as I noticed a familiar car pulling up on the forecourt.

Henry grabbed William and pushed him through a door that was obviously private. 'No, no,' cried the man behind the counter. I shoved a $100 note at him, but he was still gesturing that he would not help us. Hurling myself through the door after Henry and William I yelled at them to keep running. Luckily for us, there was a small back entrance that was unlocked. Shouts were coming from behind us in the main store. Running and half dragging William, we fled into the streets. Harad was full of tiny passageways and blind alleys. Running footsteps came up behind us. Suddenly there was a gun-shot and a bullet ricocheted off the side of a building, just above our heads. 'Keep going, don't look back,' yelled Henry, as he began returning fire with his two pistols.

I yanked William down an alleyway. 'We're dead men,' he was saying.

'Not yet. Keep going,' I snapped.

More gunfire. Henry was close behind, fending off our pursuers. Suddenly there was a shot and a blood cur-dling cry. I glanced back, still running. Henry was down. There was nothing I could do. My job was to keep William alive. We ran on, pushing through doorways and hidden courtyards, climbing low walls and burrow-ing further into the maze of sleeping residences.

'Stop, stop, I've got to stop,' gasped William. 'I can't go any further, man.' I slowed down. Henry had created a diversion and we seemed to have shaken off the men. We climbed a low wall and found ourselves in another narrow street. I felt sick with anger over Henry. 'We're not safe,' I said to William, pulling him into a thick wall of vines that were growing up a building. 'If they don't get me, a heart attack will,' William said, trying to breathe deeply. I had to work out what to do. They would expect us to try to hide in the village, rather than head out into the desert. Dare I call their bluff? How long could we survive out there? Did we have a choice? I doubted that anyone in the village would protect us.

Suddenly there was a noise. A huge Arab man came out of his house. He must have heard us. I pushed William behind me as the man pulled back the vines. Our eyes met and immediately he started shouting. I gestured frantically for him to be quiet, but he wouldn't shut up. I had no choice. I kicked him in his throat, undoubtedly bursting his windpipe. As he fell to the floor I was conscious of one of the attackers coming up the alleyway from behind. I took his first punch, knowing I needed to keep my arms free and concentrate on his other hand. He was trying to pull his gun out of his pocket. I grabbed his thumb, ripping it back so it disabled his arm. He screamed and fell to the floor. I yanked his gun from him and shot him in the head.

The area suddenly swarmed with people and I could see the other aggressors coming up quickly. I grabbed William and shot the gun in the air, sending the people running for cover.

Again we stumbled through passageways and streets until I could see the edge of the desert. 'This way!' I said to William. He didn't have the time or strength to argue. We headed out into the darkness of open land.

We continued running and stumbling through the sand for what must have been close to an hour. It stung our nostrils and clung to our legs, dragging us down as we panted and gasped at the dry air. 'Keep breathing, keep moving forward,' I encouraged William. It seemed my plan had worked. 'They're probably still combing the village for us,' I said, 'but we have to keep going.'

'How far is Bahrain?'

'You don't want to know.'

We walked in silence, keeping up as fast a pace as we could manage. I knew we'd put some good distance between us and they wouldn't be able to drive the car into the desert. Still, they wouldn't give up easily.

Before long, they would work out where we were heading.

Sure enough, I thought I heard voices in the distance behind us. We stood still, straining our eyes back over our tracks. 'It's them,' I said. William's face was consumed with fear and dread. By now the terrain had grown even more difficult. We forced our limbs to move, sliding in the thick sand. I feared there was a storm brewing. 'What's that?' asked William, as we cleared the brow of another dune. I squinted through the darkness. There were several small fires and I could just about make out the silhouettes of tents and animals.

'Bedouin.'

We had only one chance. William was flagging badly and it wouldn't be long before our pursuers caught up with us. We ran down the other side of the dune, toward the settlement.

As we reached the edge of the tented village we saw a man attending to his camels. He grinned as we approached. It was a shock. I hadn't expected a friendly face. I tried to talk to him in Arabic. Another shock. He spoke half decent English. 'What's your problem, gentlemen?' he said, still smiling as he looked us up and down.

'We're in trouble,' I gasped, still breathless from the slog. 'There are people trying to kill us.'

'Why, what have you done?'

'We've done nothing wrong . . . ' I started. I was reluctant to tell him any details. Fortunately, he held up his hand to interrupt.

'Come, come,' he said. 'You look like harmless men to me,' he grinned, ushering us towards one of the large tents. 'Tonight you will eat, drink and rest with us.' Relieved that he wasn't going to push us about our business, I looked at William and shrugged my shoulders.

William was about to pass out with exhaustion. We let the stranger lead us into one of the tents.

There were a number of men sitting smoking from a shared hookah. They stared at us when we walked in, but didn't really respond. Our friend jabbered something in Arabic and within minutes we were served with unleavened bread, cheese, honey and a spicy lentil dish.

After we'd eaten, William quickly fell asleep among the sheepskin rugs and smell of hashish. Our friend sat down beside me and introduced himself as Hashanni. I noticed that the other men retained the same stony-faced expressions at all times, but he talked animatedly, always with a broad grin. His English was remarkably good, but heavily accented, so I had to concentrate hard on what he was saying. After a while, he quietened. 'You told me you are in some sort of trouble,' he said. 'You can stay here for three days. We will protect you and ask you nothing of it.'

'Thank you . . . ' I started.

'After three days, you will tell us what is your business, or you will leave.' He paused. 'Or we will kill you. That is the way of the Bedouin.' Hashanni smiled as he told me this, but I knew he was deadly serious.

I bowed to him. 'Thank you for your generous hospitality,' I said. He laughed out loud, clapping his hands together in delight.

Exhaustion fell on me and I rested well.

The next day William and I stayed close to Hashanni, watching him as he tended the camels. I had studied many animals in my Kung Fu training, but the camel was a mystery to me. At one point I made the mistake of touching a bag of food. Before I knew what was going on, one of the camels came lunging towards me, snorting and spitting. I yelled, attempting to shoo it away, but it snapped at me, trying to bite. I began running and the

beast followed in hot pursuit. All I could hear was
laughter from William, Hashanni, and even some of the
stone faces as I shot into a nearby tent to escape.

'She thought you were going to take her food,'
explained Hashanni, still laughing, as he came in to rescue me. He had tethered the animal and she had her nose
stuck in the feeding bag. We eyed each other warily.
'Later I will teach you to ride,' he told me. I didn't relish
the idea, but it occurred to me that this might be our only
way out of the desert.

'We'll laugh about this one day,' joked William as our
steeds lumbered along in the late afternoon sun, behind
a singing Hashanni.

'Just call me Lawrence,' I said.

William and I stayed in the protection of the Bedouin for
two days. It was quite an eye-opener to see their way of
life. They were a very serious, religious people; dedicated
Muslims who prayed five times a day and gave open
thanks to Allah before every meal. Hashanni took us from
tent to tent where men, women and children were working on beautiful tapestries and other crafts to sell in the
town. We marvelled at the way they seemed to be completely self-sustaining, despite the arid desert conditions.

Our host seemed to enjoy us being around. He taught
us to ride the camels and had long conversations with
William about all kinds of business. I was mindful, however, of his warning. On the morning of the third day we
set out into the desert. A couple of hundred US dollars
had secured us a camel each and enough supplies to get
us to Qatar. Hashanni gave us details of a man we could
contact there for help. 'Feels good to be on our way
home,' said William as we neared the city. We still didn't
know what lay ahead. I wouldn't relax until we were
safely back on US soil.

'Come in, come in,' said the jolly, little rounded man who had the same smile as his Bedouin friend. Again, we were surprised to find that he spoke almost perfect English.

'Don't tell him we've parked the camels on double yellows,' whispered William, as we bowed through the low door into his shop. It smelt of incense and hashish. It was obviously some kind of travel service. We were able to make contact with Sandra and the man issued us with a couple of boat tickets from Qatar to Bahrain. 'You stay here with me tonight,' he told us. 'Set off first thing in the morning.'

'Hardly Le Meridian is it?' said William as the man left us in a grubby little room with two narrow beds. He wasn't really complaining. The Bedouin had given us water to freshen up, but it was a relief to have a shave and a decent shower and slip into relatively clean sheets.

The boat was heavily loaded with peasants and animals. The journey lasted just over an hour and we were relieved to reach Bahrain. A German man named Julian met us and took us to the safe house. There we were issued with passports, papers and airline tickets. 'It is too risky to travel the main routes,' he informed us. I looked at the tickets. Bulgarian airlines. We were to take a strange and convoluted route back to the US. I knew Sandra was behind it. Good girl. She wasn't prepared to take any more chances. According to our passports I was now an Italian businessman, Antonio Carreras. William was Walter Schmidt, from The Netherlands.

Two days later we landed safely at JFK airport, New York. William rewarded me handsomely for my work. 'I don't care if I never set foot in Saudi Arabia again,' I told him, with a wink. It was, therefore, with some irony that I soon found myself with a new assignment: firsthand man to Amin Fahed, Saudi Arabian Ambassador to the UK, Italy and Cyprus.

Chapter 7

Amin Fahed became my priority client. The IKFF sometimes pulled me away on short assignments, but Fahed
was a big deal to them. His government paid well for
his protection. Depending on his whereabouts and the
changing political climate, he was a high-risk customer.
I headed up the five-man protection unit and found
myself jetting all over the world, with extended periods
in his lavish residences in London, Naples and
Limassol.

Amin was a serious gambler who courted trouble and
didn't care. He had the power and wealth to deal with it.
He could be gracious to his debtors, but when he lost
patience he was ruthless in reclaiming his money. It was
a side of his business that the close protection team
stayed well clear of. He'd offered each one of us serious
money to do debt collection work on the side, but none
of us were foolish enough to jeopardise the position of
the IKFF. Besides, we were well funded.

By now I was one of the IKFF's highest paid bodyguards. I rented a substantial apartment in London's
Paddington where my parents lived at my expense.
Finally, it seemed, my mother had the life she had
always aspired to.

In the summer of 1987 I took a couple of weeks' leave
from Amin's service. He was as safe as he could be, at
home in Saudi Arabia, and I returned to London. I knew
my father would appreciate my being around. He could

rarely leave the apartment these days. I also looked forward to catching up with some old friends.

It was a beautiful summer morning when I met my Chinese friend, Gerry, in Hyde Park. He was a student of martial arts who I had met at Mr Chang's school. Taking a boat out on the lake, Gerry was happy to row as I lay back, enjoying the sun on my face.

'Hey, Tony, get a load of this.' I sat up, squinting in the sunlight. There were three blonde girls in a boat, not too far away. They had dropped one of the oars in the lake and two of them were hanging over the edge of the boat, trying to reach it. There was a great deal of giggling and shouting. We watched, in amusement, as their splashing propelled the boat further away. 'I don't believe it,' laughed Gerry, as one of the girls tried to reach the estranged oar using the other one. The boat was rocking and she was laughing so much that she soon lost hold of the second oar, leaving them stranded, floating adrift in the middle of the lake. 'C'mon Gerry,' I said, with great relish, 'time to go to the rescue.'

'Ah, knights in shining armour,' one of the girls laughed as we drew up to them. I was sure they had been talking to each other in some kind of Scandinavian language, but they spoke English to us. We had no intention of collecting the oars for them. Much better that they got in our boat. Still giggling, they agreed, introducing themselves as sisters, Leah, Lena and Aiya. Both boats rocked dangerously as Leah clambered aboard. She then turned and offered her hand to Aiya, who was crouching in the boat, clinging nervously to the side. Lena seemed to be offering overcautious guidance from behind. It was then I realised that Aiya was blind. As the weight shifted both boats rocked precariously and I feared she might lose her step. Leah squealed and fell backwards, landing on Gerry amid raucous laughter. Catching her raised arm, I put a hand on her waist and pulled Aiya safely into our boat. In that moment something happened to me. I held her close for only a fraction of a second, but I was left strangely breathless. She was exquisite: mysterious in her blindness and beauty. Seating her beside me, I offered my hand to Lena, but Gerry was already there.

We took a long route back to the river bank and the girls insisted we join them for a drink, by way of thanks. We took no persuading. Gerry, Lena and Leah jumped out of the boat and I stood behind to help Aiya. I felt nervous and uncertain. Not knowing how to handle her, I positioned myself to lift her, as I would my father. Her sisters giggled. 'Steady,' she gasped and, manoeuvring me in front of her, she put a hand on my shoulder and motioned me to lead the way. Using my step as a guide, she strode confidently onto the bank. Her right hand did not leave my shoulder, but now she moved around in front of me and began running her left hand over my face. I smiled nervously, looking into two beautiful, deep blue eyes that could not see. She started at my forehead and, with gentle, but firm fingers, ran her hands across my eyes and down over my nose. They lingered at my lips, then traced my jawline, resting lightly on my chin. 'Hmmm, you're really good looking,' she said mischievously. I was astonished at her forthrightness.

'Are you flirting with me?' I laughed.

She linked her arm through mine and we followed the others.

We spent ages over coffee and cheesecake and learned that Lena and Leah were visiting from their home in Sweden. To my all too obvious astonishment, Aiya was a first year law student in London. 'I'm blind, not stupid,' she said indignantly. Then she smiled, enjoying my embarrassment as I stumbled with profuse apologies and futile attempts to compensate my insensitivity.

That night I took Aiya to one of my favourite Dim Sum restaurants in Chinatown. In the days ahead we quickly became inseparable. Something very special was happening between us. Flirtatious flings and the odd torrid affair were not unknown to me. They came with the territory. This was different. Aiya seemed to be able to see deep into my soul. I didn't understand how she could reach me in that way. She came from a wonderful, loving family and seemed to have no cares in the world. Despite her blindness, her face shone with confidence and self-assurance. Yet, from somewhere in the depths of her being, she reached out to a loneliness and despair that I had never even acknowledged in myself. It was unnerving. In tasting love, I was opening up a whole gamut of other emotions. I battled hard. It would have been easy to push her away, but she had a strange hold on me. Still, there were dark places in my soul that I would not let myself, never mind anyone else, enter.

Returning to my assignments was tough, but I was thankful that Amin's work brought us back to London for extended periods. I was really happy for the first time in my life.

For the next three years Aiya and I saw each other as much as we could. I spent holidays with her and the family at their home in Stockholm. It was there that I first found myself on the wrong side of the law. I should have known from my studies in criminal law that it is illegal to use martial arts in certain countries. I had gone out alone to buy cigarettes, when I heard screaming coming from the wooded area near Aiya's parents' house. I ran into the nearby shop and shouted at the man behind the counter to call the police. Outside, the screaming had become muffled cries. I belted into the trees. To my horror I saw a woman wresting beneath a man. He had his trousers undone and was punching her and pulling at her clothing. Immediately I leapt onto him. Yanking him away I continued to beat him as the battered woman gathered herself together. The next thing I knew, I was being tackled to the ground.

'Halt! Polis! Stop!'

The sergeant held me in a judo grip. I offered no resistance and watched as two other officers arrested the rapist. The woman sat by a tree, sobbing uncontrollably and pulling her ripped clothing around her. She seemed to be bleeding badly. I wanted to comfort her, but the policeman would not loosen his hold. Surely he realised what had happened? Finally he let me stand. To my astonishment, however, he then arrested me and I was taken, along with the rapist, to the local police station.

I explained as much as I could in my basic Swedish, but it was a relief when Aiya and her father arrived at the station. There was quite a heated debate between her father and the police sergeant. I struggled to understand what was being said. 'He is saying that he is sympathetic to you,' whispered Aiya, in translation, 'but that you have broken the law. It is not legal to use martial arts in this country.' I was livid.

'But what about that poor woman?' I asked angrily.

'That is what my father is saying to him. You saved her from a truly dreadful fate.'

'They see that?'

'Oh yes, but he keeps repeating that the law is the law.'

Finally the police sergeant came over to me. He spoke slowly, in Swedish, giving me an official warning before telling me I was free to go. Aiya's father shook his hand in thanks.

'That was close,' he said to me, as we left. 'You were about to spend the night in the cells.'

Aiya was supportive, but I knew she worried about my work. I, too, was aware that the risks were high. I could be killed at any time. Was I being fair to her? Aiya was beginning to talk of getting married. I loved her deeply and spending time with her parents and sisters made me realise what I had missed over the years. I yearned for a normal, loving family life. Perhaps one day we might even have children of our own. Maybe it was time to change my lifestyle.

I had to return to Naples to prepare for my next assignment with Amin. I had an apartment there which I shared with William and Kevin, a couple of professional basketball players. They, too, were funded by the IKFF.

William took the call. He was a giant of a man, a black dude from Chicago who was always playing tricks. I was aware that he was on the telephone, but I was so engrossed in a film that I didn't pick up on the tone of his voice. Suddenly he switched off the TV and stood in front me. 'Tony man, I've got some tough news for you. Aiya's been in an accident . . . '

He told me Aiya had been killed in a car crash in London. Joyriders had overtaken a lorry and run head on into her friend's car. Everyone was killed instantly.

Anger rose within me. 'What?! Who was that, why didn't they speak to me, what are you talking about?' I didn't know what to think. I swore viciously at William and lashed out with my foot to his chest. He went crashing to the floor. I wouldn't believe him. 'This is one of your sick jokes,' I yelled at him, cursing and calling him every name under the sun. But I knew inside that he was telling the truth. Even William wouldn't joke about something like this.

In the days following it was as though something had snapped inside me. My anger was uncontrollable. One night I went out on my motorbike, driving like a madman until I was pursued by two police officers. Everything within me wanted to drive them into the ground, or over the mountain's edge. I didn't care if I lived or died. I raced on with the officers in hot pursuit. Finally, I calmed myself and pulled to a stop. The officers were furious. Gritting my teeth, I showed them my diplomat's card and said nothing. They were breathless after the chase. 'Come on, make me hit you,' I thought, the rage burning within me. They examined the card and climbed back on their bikes in resignation. My diplomatic secure status meant they could not touch me.

My friends didn't know how to handle the rage that consumed me. They kept out of my way. They weren't the kind of guys to have heart-to-hearts. One evening, William tried his best to talk to me. I threatened to smash his face in.

Heading out, I stumbled into a small, dimly-lit club, just off the main street in Naples town centre. I wanted to be alone, to sit, to think, to hide. I went up to the bar and asked for a glass of milk. The barman laughed, but seeing the aggression in my eyes he turned serious. Again, I said, 'Just give me the milk, and take my money.' I pushed a note at him.

'I can't serve you milk.'

'Then I'll take a juice.'

'You don't understand,' he said, pointing to a sign above his head. 'A beer at 5,000 Lira, or a bottle of champagne at 12,000. Then you get the girl.'

'Girl? What girl. I don't want no girl. Just give me a drink.' I didn't realise what he was saying, I just wanted to sit down.

'Will that be beer or champagne?'

'Just give me a beer!' I demanded, seconds away from hitting him. I took the beer, which I had no intention of drinking, over to a table in the furthest corner of the bar. I had been there only a few minutes when a girl came over and sat down opposite. She was obviously quite young, but wore heavy make-up and an almost over-powering scent. I looked at her, wondering what she was about.

'What do you want?' I demanded.

'Will you buy me a drink?' came her reply. I was a little taken aback. She looked at me through thick black eyelashes and smiled from the corner of her mouth. I was irritated.

'OK, what do you want?'

'Champagne.'

'What a cheek!' I thought, but I couldn't be bothered arguing and signalled to the barman. To my indignant surprise, he brought over a bottle of champagne and left it at the table with a bill for 17,000 Lira.

'What do you want to talk about?' asked the girl, seductively. I was getting angry.

'I don't really want to talk to you.'

Now she was taken aback. 'Well why did you buy the champagne?'

'Because you asked me for a drink.'

As I spoke, I began to understand what was going on.

'You paid for that drink so you could talk to me,' she was saying.

I was horrified. 'I've made a mistake. I just want to be alone,' I said, getting up to leave.

'No please, don't!' There was desperation in her voice. 'So you don't want to sleep with me?'

'No!' I began to move again, but she grabbed my hand.

'Please, I'm happy just to talk. Don't do this to me.' She looked nervously in the direction of the bar. I didn't know what to do. I wanted to be alone, but I felt sorry for the girl. If I left now, where would I go? I couldn't be bothered to think about it. We stayed in the bar together for a couple of hours, under the glaring eye of the bar manager.

The next day I walked into a local coffee shop and was startled to see the same girl, sitting at a table biting her fingernails and pretending to read a magazine. I had to look twice. It had been dark in the bar the previous evening, but I recognised the same tarty clothes, the scent and heavy make-up. She smiled to see me, then looked ashamed. I ordered two coffees and joined her at the table. The previous evening I had told her something of my life and about Aiya and the accident. Now it was her turn. She told me her name was Rosanna and that she had come from Romania. She had wanted to go to college, but now she was working as a prostitute. She hated the work and was terribly ashamed. Soon she was fighting to stop her tears.

'Why do you do this?' I asked.

'Because they own me,' she replied. 'My parents sold me before I was 16. They couldn't afford to keep me at home.'

'But why don't you leave? Just walk away.'

'I can't, I told you, they own me. They have my passport and I have no money.'

'No one owns you. I will help you get away.'

For the first time since Aiya's death my mind wasn't consumed by my own problems. I remembered my cousin, Siu Ming, who had been snatched and forced to work in a brothel in Shanghai. I had no time for anyone who mistreated women in this way. As she talked, Rosanna twisted a gold band round and round on her middle finger. I promised to help her. She took off the ring and insisted I take it. It just fit on my little finger. She scribbled an address on a cigarette paper and left.

Later that afternoon I went on my motorbike to a tenement block, just around the corner from the bar where I had first met Rosanna. She was waiting for me outside. She could barely speak for nerves, but I was ready for action. We took the stairs up to a long corridor of rooms. Some of the doors were open and I could see girls laying on beds, asleep or reading magazines. Some of them whistled as we walked by. There were a couple of large, tough-looking men patrolling the corridor and one came towards me, asking my business. I was obviously not expected to be there at that time of day. His attitude angered me. I said nothing, but kicked him to the floor and pushed my knee deep into his face until the bones cracked.

The other bouncer came rushing down the corridor, only to suffer a similar fate. Rosanna grabbed a small bag of belongings from her room, then led me downstairs to the manager's office. He was a weedy, weasel of a man. I demanded he give Rosanna her passport and, seeing I meant business, he immediately began rifling through a drawer until he found her papers. He put up no resistance, but I smashed his face into the desktop until blood splattered up onto my clothes. It felt good. I spotted the steel letter opener he had been using, and raised it, intending to stab him. Just then, I realised Rosanna was watching me. I stopped and threw the instrument across the room. Grabbing her hand, I dragged the girl out of the building, onto my bike and swiftly headed for my apartment.

Rosanna was still shaking as I opened the door. Her face had been filled with terror back in the manager's office. I knew what she must have been thinking. I tried to reassure her. I was not normally violent in that way. I talked more about what had happened to me over the last few weeks. Gradually, she started to relax and I showed her through to my bedroom.

'You have been so good to me,' she said. 'I have to repay you.' She took my face in her hands and began to raise her mouth to mine.

'No!'

'But, it's all I can do. I have no money.'

'I don't want any money. I don't want anything from you.' I guided her to the bed and grabbed a spare blanket from the wardrobe. 'Call if there is anything you need. I will be here on the sofa in the lounge,' I said, nervously backing out of the room.

The next day I took Rosanna to the airport and bought her a ticket home. She wore jeans, a big sweater and no make-up. She was quite beautiful. 'I will never be able to thank you enough,' she said. I handed her an envelope containing a wad of notes.

'Now, make sure you enrol at a decent college,' I told her, feeling strangely fatherly. Tears welled up in her eyes. She kissed me softly on my cheek and I watched as she walked away.

Driving back towards town I relived the previous day's events and the way I had brutalised the men. It felt so good. I wanted to beat them till their bodies burst, till I tasted their blood in my mouth. With every smash I felt something of my rage was leaving me, but I wanted more. Riding more and more recklessly I squeezed my eyes shut to rid myself of the images. I was consumed by shame, yet there was a new hunger in me, something evil, something addictive and uncontrollable. I spun the bike around, leaned on the throttle and headed into the hills.

Chapter 8

I could not bear to be alone. Neither did I want company. I spent my time in bars and clubs, watching the happy, smiling, carefree people. I didn't want to talk to anyone. The noise of the bar helped smother my pain, but in the depths of my subconscious, there was another, far more sinister reason why I chose these places. I still had a strange sensation in my mouth. It was the same metallic taste that I first experienced when beating up the man in Rosanna's brothel. I tried to forget it. But there it was again. It was the taste of my rage, a ferocious and extremely tangible thirst for blood. It was as though, overnight, I was a changed man. The discipline of my vocation disappeared and I was hungry for confrontation.

The IKFF offered me some time out, but Amin Fahed was anxious to have me back at work. He contacted me directly, requesting that I meet him at his new base in Lefkosia, Cyprus. I was all too ready to accept the assignment.

On my first night off I headed for the nightlife of Nicosia. Afrikanas was a lively, packed bar, but I found a stool in a secluded corner and sat back to watch the people. There was a large group of Danish soldiers. I watched them in disdain as each one was challenged to throw back their drink whilst his mates chanted and clapped. Most chose spirits, but one man, a thickly-built brute, over six feet tall, got the biggest cheers downing six pints of beer, one after the other.

'Idiots,' I thought. 'I'd like to teach them a lesson or two, see how tough they really are.' I watched the soldiers becoming drunk and more raucous with each passing hour. In one of the booths there were three girls, chatting and enjoying a drink together. I couldn't help think of Aiya and her sisters. One of them was blonde and fair skinned, just like her. They were minding their own business, but the soldiers were beginning to show interest. When the blonde girl got up to go to the bar she was followed by one of them. My blood began to boil as I watched the girl trying to politely shun his advances. As she waited to be served the soldier grew more persistent. She turned her back on him, but he still would not leave her alone. I sat forward on my seat, keeping a close eye on them as he moved around in front of her. She turned again and this time he grabbed her shoulder, pulling her roughly back to face him. I could see the fear in her face as she struggled to get away.

Anger and hatred rose within me. With no more thought I walked up to the bar, smashed my glass and stuck it in the soldier's face.

There was uproar. Ten or twelve soldiers rushed at the bar. Using a speedy coiling snake move I slipped between them and flew up the steps, out into the brightly lit street. I had gained myself some vital space. The soldiers were heavily inebriated and I knew I could easily take them all, but not in the confines of the small club.

'C'mon. Come and get it!' I yelled. Adrenaline pumped around my body, hungry for the fight. As each soldier emerged from the darkness I hit him with a stop punch to the face or groin, sending him flying to the floor. One managed a strike at my head but as the pain burned around my eye it fed my rage. It wasn't enough to lay them out. I wanted to cause some serious damage.

Bloodthirsty, I launched into them, smashing noses, cracking bones and hurting them any way I could.

In the heat of my rage I felt the excited walloping of my own veins and arteries as each punch fed my hunger. I wanted more and more.

Then, suddenly, police sirens. I fled into the night.

'So I hear you enjoyed a bit of a rumble last night,' said Amin with a wink and an ear-to-ear grin.

'Nothing I couldn't handle,' I said, smoothing the tender skin around my right eye. It irritated me that he'd heard about it already. Then again, he was a very powerful man. He was sly and shrewd and knew how to operate.

Amin obviously recognised a change in me that he thought could work to his advantage. 'Tonight is play time,' he announced, clapping his hands and unlocking the safe to pull out several thick piles of banknotes, secured with elastic bands.

The casino was busy and just about everyone greeted Amin with a respectful nod or handshake as we walked through the private lounge. 'Ah, Mr Fahed, you are feeling lucky tonight, yes?' said the manager, as he personally escorted us to Amin's favourite table. Amin smiled to himself. Self-assured pleasure and greed swept over his face as the croupier dealt the cards. The game was just about to begin when a man came over and started talking to him. He was agitated and I could see my boss growing more irritated by his presence. I waited until Amin gave me the nod, then went over and stood very close. The man was clearly intimidated, but he kept on at Amin, talking faster and more desperately. I didn't need to wait for a signal. As the man reached out to touch Amin's arm I hauled him away and knocked him to the floor. I didn't need to do any more. He picked himself up and ran. Amin gave me a nod of approval and continued his game.

The next day my boss summoned me to his penthouse. He was extra friendly and I knew what was coming. This time I was ready to accept.

That night I paid a visit to a man who had a large outstanding debt with Amin. He was a notorious arms dealer. I had caught him off guard. His staff had left for the evening and he was alone in the house. I told him I had come to collect the money he owed to Mr Fahed. He smiled, the same confident, arrogant smile that adorned the faces of many of my rich and powerful clients. It sickened me. Who did he think he was?

'Tell your boss that I do not have the money,' he said. 'It will be delivered to him in full by the end of next week.' With that, he showed me the door. I was irritated, but I reminded myself, this was not my fight.

Amin was spitting with anger. 'Go back and make him pay me tonight,' he ordered. 'When he pays, hurt him anyway!' Though I didn't appreciate being addressed in this way, I had immense loyalty to Amin. The IKFF paid me to protect him, but it went deeper than that. Perhaps it had something to do with my upbringing. My sole motivation was the satisfaction of my client. Amin was asking me to go way beyond the IKFF's remit but now I was willing to cross the line. It enraged me that anyone should think they could disrespect and mess around with the honour of my client in this way. I returned to the house and did as I was asked.

Amin was more than satisfied and rewarded me handsomely, but I took greater pleasure from the violence of the work. Once again, it had fed the sickening craving for violence that burned madly within me.

Back in the casino my anger raged as I watched Chad, a large African man, flaunting his money. Swaggering around the room, he ordered champagne for anyone he talked to and pushed folded notes down the tops of the scantly-dressed serving girls who pandered to his every whim. He was well known to me. He owed Amin a large sum of money from a gambling debt. That night I went to his house.

It was a large residence and when the butler would not let me in I kicked the door down. Knocking the terrified man to the floor, I barged my way into Chad's sitting room. He began to protest, telling me I had no right to come to his house. He didn't get the chance to finish his sentence. I grabbed him by his hair, hurting him until he took me to a large safe, encased within a wall of bookshelves. Helping myself to the money, I pushed him against the wall and continued beating him, relishing the snapping of his bones and the smell of his blood. Just then, two children came running into the room, screaming hysterically, 'Papa, Papa!' Their wailing brought me to my senses. I let him drop and he collapsed in a twisted heap on the floor. I pushed past them and fled.

Outside, I was high with the thrill of the beating and let out a triumphant yell as the bike tyres squealed. The images of the children flashed into my head, but I forced them away and drew in my breath. I savoured the smell of fresh blood lingering in my nostrils.

There were several other such incidents and the beatings I gave grew more brutal each time. I knew there would be retribution for Amin, that one day a hitman would be employed to track him down in a counter-attack. I was also aware that the IKFF would deal with me very severely if they found out what I was up to. The only way to prevent this was to ensure the people I attacked were so scared, or physically damaged that they would not, or could not speak of it.

Back home my parents remained as ignorant and disinterested as ever in my life. It infuriated me that they never even mentioned Aiya's name. It was as though she had never existed. Still, I visited them every time I was in London and tried to make life as comfortable as possible for them. One evening my mother announced that there was the possibility of some new treatment for my father's condition. 'Of course, we don't have that kind of money,' she said. 'We need around £30,000 to send your father for tests in Switzerland. We thought you might be able . . . ' I looked at my father's face. For the first time in years, there was a look of hope and he smiled weakly. I was well paid, but I didn't have anything like that kind of money put by.

'I will see what I can do,' I told them.

Touching down in Cyprus my mind was set on how I might get the money. I could have gone to Amin, but I didn't want to be in debt to anyone. I didn't need to be. By now, I had lost all respect for people and their property. Working for Amin, I had become a merciless debt collector and thief. I realigned my focus. My goal was to get the money for my father's operation. It would be easy. I knew the wealthiest people in the area and it wasn't hard to select a target.

I made my choice. He wasn't a nice man anyway. He deserved it. That night I broke into his house and took all the money I could find, delivering a brutal beating when I was disturbed. I hadn't intended hurting anyone, but the fight was a bonus for me. It left me high and hungry for more. I was invincible. Back in the town, I walked determinedly into one of the five star hotels.

'Room 507,' I demanded confidently, having quickly scanned the key rack. The receptionist gave me the key.

'Have a good evening, sir.'

I headed for the elevator and soon emerged on the fifth floor. 'This is too easy,' I thought as I let myself into the room and began rifling through the drawers. I quickly found what I wanted. Whoever these people were, they had plenty of spending money. I took it all, then moved on to the next hotel, and the next.

Now I took more notice of which keys were at the desk. I asked for the key to one room and, after robbing it, climbed out onto the balcony and made my way across to another, knowing its occupants were out. I slid the glass doors open and eased my way in. As I began my hunt for money, I was suddenly startled by voices and the sound of the key being inserted into the lock. Ducking back behind the curtain, I quietened my breathing. A young man and woman came in. They had no idea I was there. What would I do if they came to the window? The metallic taste rose again in my mouth. The couple were happy, giggling and starting to get very amorous with one another. I had their money. There was no need to hurt them. Quietly, I slipped out through the balcony doors, pulling them shut behind me before lowering myself onto the balcony below. In that one night I collected the money I needed for my father.

A few days later I flew my parents out to Cyprus and gave them the money. They were delighted. They stayed in my apartment for a short break before returning to London to prepare for the treatment.

Leaving my parents at the airport, I headed into Limassol where I'd arranged to meet a couple of friends. It was a hot evening and the town was lively with holiday-makers and touts selling timeshares. We swapped stories over coffee and watched the world go by. Before long a group of English people came along and set up a large wooden cross, just a short distance away. 'Oh no, Christians,' scoffed Kevin, my Canadian friend. The group began playing guitars and singing and he continued to mock them. 'Bible-bashers, they're the same the world over.' I laughed, but I had no real problem with them, so long as they didn't bother me. When they finished singing, one of the men started to speak. He had a loud voice and despite the sneers and jibes of many passers-by he continued to address a small gathering crowd. Holding a bottle in his hand, he called out, 'Who wants this bottle of wine?' There were no takers. 'C'mon, there's no catch. It's just a bottle of wine. It's yours for free, a gift.'

'Nutcase,' said Kevin. 'C'mon, let's get out of here.' I, too, sneered at the preacher, but I was happy to stay and finish my coffee. Kevin was heading off to a club to meet some of the timeshare agents. I hated that crowd. They were full of themselves and never shut up about their work.

'Go ahead, I'll catch you later,' I told him. The preacher continued to offer his bottle of wine to the crowd. He was a man about my age with longish hair, dressed in a T-shirt and Bermuda shorts. 'Probably a student,' I thought. Eventually a middle-aged woman approached tentatively.

'Here, I'll take it,' she said.

The crowd watched in expectation as the preacher handed her the bottle.

'See, no strings attached. It's just a free gift,' he repeated. 'All you have to do is step forward and take it.'

The woman took her place in the crowd as the preacher got to the heart of his message. 'This is just like Jesus' gift of salvation,' he said. 'Jesus loves us all and his gift of salvation is free. All we have to do is take it. God is not a God who will force anything on us. It's up to us to step forward.'

My mind went back to Mr Sizer, my RE teacher at school. I remember him explaining this word 'salvation', that it meant wiping away all the bad things in life, being forgiven so we can start again and be clean before God. 'He'd have some serious scrubbing to do with me,' I thought sadly.

Eventually, the crowd dispersed and the Christians began packing their things away. At one point the preacher caught my eye and came over. 'Can I join you?' he asked.

'Sure.' I wondered what he was up to, but he seemed a nice enough guy and I was quite intrigued. He introduced himself as Martin. We chatted for a while, mainly about what the group was doing. They had come to work with a local church in Limassol for a couple of months and had only just arrived a few days ago. I gave him some hints and tips about the area and soon found myself telling him a little about why I was in Cyprus.

'You must come round and meet Michael Wright,' he told me. 'He's a great guy. He's from Northern Ireland, but he lives here now. You two would really get on.'

There was something about Martin. He seemed genuine. He talked about himself, the group and about God. I couldn't work out his agenda. It wasn't as though he was hiding anything. He told me up front that he was a Christian and he wanted everyone to know about Jesus and how much he loves us all. I wasn't really interested in all that religious rubbish, but Martin seemed like a decent sort. He obviously just wanted to help people. I didn't mix with anyone like that. When his friends began to leave, Martin got up, as if to go. Realising how much I had enjoyed his company, I held out my hand to say goodbye. He hesitated. 'Look, we're all heading back to our apartment, why don't you join us for a takeaway?' he asked. I was quite taken aback. Rarely did I get invited into someone's home. I was intrigued and

accepted his offer. I would go along and if it was anything dodgy I would beat them all up, I decided.

The rented apartment was like many of the holiday
lets in Limassol and Martin introduced me to the rest of
the team. They were all young people and very welcoming. I was relieved that they didn't make too much fuss
over me or ask me too many questions. We ate together
and the conversation remained light and fun. There was
something fresh and appealing about them. A few of
them mentioned this guy Michael Wright. 'Come to our
church,' they said. 'You'll meet him there.' I promised I'd
think about it. I left them with a smile on my face and
thought maybe I would seek them out again. For now, it
was time to catch up with Kevin and some serious club
action.

I never did get to their church. A few days later I was
walking along the street when a police car pulled up
alongside me. Two officers got out, showing me their
identity badges. 'Get into the car,' one of them
demanded.

I swore at him. 'You can't touch me,' I told him, flashing my diplomat's pass.

He pulled out a pistol. I looked at it and laughed. It
was an ancient-looking thing, probably incapable of
firing.

'OK, if that's how you want to play it,' I sneered. 'Take
me to your police station, and watch me walk straight
out.' I wasn't worried and decided to play along. I
didn't have much else to do that afternoon.

Once in the station, my diplomatic immunity counted
for nothing. I was quickly incarcerated in a dungeon-
type cell. My demands to contact someone at the British
embassy were ignored. I heard nothing until 10 o'clock
in the evening when a group of uniformed policemen
came into the cell. They handcuffed me and led me

upstairs to an interview room. 'This is where it will end,' I thought. 'They will charge me, release me on bail, then I'll get out of the country.' By then, I was beginning to worry that they might be able to pin something on me, given enough time.

On the desk there was a huge pile of files. The officer in charge opened the first few and began asking questions. Each file represented a hotel room that had been robbed. I admitted to knowing about the first few, but there were many more files and details of which I knew nothing. When I began denying my involvement in them the officer grew irritated. He wanted a full confession that would wrap up the whole pile. There was no way I was going to admit to crimes I hadn't committed. He wouldn't let up. Beads of sweat were forming on his brow and around his dirty moustache. The interrogation grew more heated and I knew he was trying to catch me out. It would be safer to keep quiet.

'I'm not saying anymore until I get my phone call,' I told him.

He scoffed and rubbed at his oily neck.

'I demand to see someone from the embassy.'

Instantly, he raised his right arm and smashed me across the face with an open palm. 'You demand nothing of me. The embassy doesn't want to see the likes of you. You're in my country now and you're in big trouble,' he spat, coming up close to my face.

Anger fired up within me. 'You son of a bitch!' I snarled, tasting the blood of my split lip. No one would make an idiot of me like this. The cuffs bit into my flesh as I took a high kick to his head, sending him flying across the room. The rest of the men instantly set about me, slapping, punching and kicking. Bracing myself, I took each blow.

Back in my cell I thought over my situation. Perhaps I really was in trouble. Surely Amin would hear of this and get me out of here? I saw no one until 10 o'clock the next evening. Again, the same policemen came for me. This time they shackled my legs as well as my arms. I refused to talk and took another severe beating.

The same thing happened for several nights, each time the beatings growing more brutal. It had become a sport to the policemen. They seemed to be growing in number. It wasn't just me they were beating. I heard conversations from other prisoners in nearby holding cells. It seemed some poor souls were suffering terrible torture. Each night the interrogation was led by the same greasy officer who tried to get me to admit to crimes I had not committed. He barked orders to his henchmen and they prepared me for the onslaught. Tearing off my shoes they put my feet through the hole in the back of a chair. A guard sat on my legs, and the officer grinned wickedly at me. Slowly he raised up his truncheon, then he smashed it down with full force into the soles of my feet. Waves of agony exploded through my legs and back. It was a form of torture I had studied as part of my training. The so-called 'bastinado' had been abolished by the Geneva convention under a war crimes act, but that meant nothing to these men. I gritted my teeth. Again, the officer pulled back the truncheon. I tried to pull back, but the blow came smashing down. 'Just give me one break and I'll kill you all.' I thought. The beating continued until I began to feel faint with pain. Finally, they pulled the chair from under me. My burning feet crashed to the stone floor. In a final burst of pain, they submerged them in icy water to prevent tell tale bruising. After seven nights of such torture, I could barely walk.

There was little point in fighting back. I was heavily chained and there were more than eight men at a time enjoying the show. What would they think of next?

Cramming a crash helmet on my head, they picked me up like a battering ram and ran me into the metal lockers. Blinding flashes exploded in my eyes until I began to lose consciousness. I cursed them as they let me crash to the floor, their leering faces grinning down at me. I tried to pull myself up but immediately I was clubbed between my legs. My whole body screamed.

By now, I didn't care if I lived or died and began deliberately antagonising them. One came at me with a metal food blender. 'Hold out your hand,' he demanded as the blade flew around in high-pitched fury. 'Forget the hand, put it to my face,' I spat. The men were frantic with excitement, but the officer in charge had had enough. 'I'm done with you, Anthony,' he screamed as he shook open the barrel of his ancient pistol. 'See this. This is yours.' He rammed a bullet into my face, before loading it into the gun. The men were immediately silent. I didn't give a damn.

'Come on then, do it, if you've got the guts,' I goaded.

I was happy to die. Since losing Aiya my life was a meaningless pit of misery and the bullet would be a welcome relief. I wouldn't allow him the satisfaction of seeing me tremble and kept my eyes fixed on his. I'd play his little game of Russian roulette like the strong man I was. The officer slowed the pace, expecting that I would plead for my life. An eerie silence crept over the room. Sweat was pouring from his face as he held the gun, now with two hands to stem the shakes of his fury. I knew exactly where the bullet was.

'Come on you gutless Greek bastard! I'm ready to gamble,' I spat at him. With a spewing torrent of abuse he rammed the pistol barrel into the back of my mouth, ulcerating my throat.

A sharp click. I didn't flinch. He slammed the gun to the floor and stormed out of the room.

I had to get out of this mess. By the time the morning officer delivered breakfast I had scraped my hands so badly on the archaic handcuffs that they were dripping with blood. He looked scared. 'I told you, they're beating me. You have to get me some medical help,' I pleaded. He was a decent man, not one of the night-time henchmen. I just had to convince him to get me to a hospital. An hour later I was in the custody of two uniformed officers.

At the hospital the handcuffs were removed and my wounds treated. Thick bandages were placed around my wrists, so the cuffs could not be replaced. My plan was working. I almost felt sorry for the two officers as they led me out, each holding one of my arms. Within moments, a speedy back flip secured my freedom. 'Stop, or I'll shoot!' As the policemen fumbled for their guns I did a coiling cobra run, zigzagging across the street. They never did fire.

Before long, the wail of police sirens filled the air. It was quiet in that area of Limassol and there were few people out on the streets. Taking no chances I made my way to a rooftop and silently settled myself, waiting for night to fall. Below, policemen were making door-to-door enquiries and officers were deployed to search the area. I remained hidden. Sitting in the darkness I began thinking over the last few months. Grief suddenly overwhelmed me. What had I become? What was I doing? A strange sense of need seemed to fill my soul, yet there was still the anger, the lust to lash out, to hurt, to taste blood. I pushed my fists into my eyes, trying to block out the torture of my thoughts and fell into light and fitful sleep.

Before first light I stole quietly back into my apartment.

Holding the receiver close to my ear I held my breath, waiting for the long-distance connection. The familiar London tone rang out. 'Come on, come on, where are you?' It was only 8 o'clock in the morning and my parents never went out before lunchtime. Minutes ticked by. Putting the phone down, I sat with my head in my hands, trying to think. It wouldn't be long before the police caught up with me. I had to talk to my mother and father. Where were they? Why weren't they answering the phone?

A couple of hours went by as I tried repeatedly to reach them.

'Mrs Downing, this is Tony Anthony, I'm sorry to trouble you.' There was a pause as my parents' neighbour realised who I was. 'Ah, yes, Tony, in Cyprus. How are you?'

'I'm trying to reach my parents, but there's no answer from the flat. Do you know where they are?' Another pause. 'Mrs Downing?'

'Tony, they are gone.'

'Gone?'

'They moved out a few days ago. We thought you must know. I still have the spare key. They've left some things of yours in the flat, but otherwise it's empty,' she said. I felt as though I had been kicked in the stomach.

'Where have they gone?'

'I'm sorry Tony . . . '

'You have no address? They must have left something.'

'No, they didn't even say goodbye. A van came and they were gone.'

I put the receiver down and swallowed hard to stop the rising in my throat. The anger in my soul began crushing me and I slammed my fists three times into the wall to try to level my mind. After everything I'd done for them, how could they do this to me?

In the next few hours I felt as though I was drowning in a sea of loneliness. It was as though my parents, abandoning me all over again, brought the true misery of my life to the fore. All the years of unspoken repression and the grief of losing Aiya now boiled in my blood and began suffocating me from inside. I lit one cigarette after another, dragging deeply and desperately on each. In fits of rage I beat my fists into the furniture and cursed my rotten parents, my stinking life.

The frenzy was broken by the sound of the doorbell.

Chapter 9

Without thinking, I opened the door. A gun barrel was pushed straight at my face.

'Stand still!'

I immediately came to my senses as I recognised the good policeman who had helped me get medical treatment the previous day.

'Why did you run, Tony?' he asked. He seemed to be alone. The police hadn't expected me to be at the apartment. I could have easily broken away, but I just looked at him wearily. 'I told you. They're beating me.'

'You know I have to take you back.' There was almost a softness in his voice and he held out handcuffs, more in a gesture, than with any force. 'If you run, I will shoot you,' he said. I held out my wrists. I was tired. 'Please, just stop the beatings and get someone from the embassy.'

'I'll see if I can do something,' he said as he led me down to his car.

I learned later that he had kept his promise. It wasn't long before several of the key henchmen lost their jobs. That first night back, however, I was still subjected to the 10 o'clock treatment. The hefty officer came in with a slow, insolent swagger. 'So, Mr Anthony. You are back in my care. Don't you worry. We look after you very well.' With that he dealt me a swift backhand slap across my face. 'You are ready to talk now, eh?' I stared at the ground and said nothing. The beating started. There was no bastinado, but I was slapped, beaten and pulled around by my hair. Finally, they propped my limp body back on the chair and offered me a cigarette. I turned away. 'Come, come. I am a reasonable man,' he said, in his slimy Greek drawl. He lit a cigarette and pushed it between my lips. I instantly spat it out. Another beating.

Finally, I decided to co-operate. It was little to do with their punishment. I was simply tired and beyond caring. All I could do was think of my parents and the way they had abandoned me. I hated them more than ever.

I admitted to all the robberies I had committed, and more besides.

A few days later, a man from the British embassy turned up. He was a well-spoken Englishman, wearing a light suit and designer shades.

'What took you so long?' I demanded angrily.

He offered me a Marlborough. 'We were told you did-n't want to see anyone.'

My hands trembled as I lit the cigarette.

'What do you mean? I've been asking for you every day since they pulled me in.'

'We learnt of your arrest, but they told us you were refus-ing help,' he repeated. 'There was nothing we could do.'

I could hardly believe it. 'I'm sorry,' he continued. 'We got a call only yesterday from someone who said you might be ready to talk.'

As I told him of my treatment, he adjusted the knot in his silk tie and shifted uncomfortably on his seat. 'We will try our best for you,' he promised, 'but you have committed serious crimes. The Greeks will not be sym-pathetic.' We sat a few moments in silence. 'We might be able to get you a lawyer, but there's no guarantee,' he told me. 'Hopefully your court hearing will be within the next three days.'

With that, I was led back to a holding cell. 'Good after-noon my friend,' said a voice from within, as the officer opened the cell door. I was surprised to hear English. A middle-aged Nigerian man got up from where he had been reading a book, and shook my hand. I was in no mood to be friendly but, relieved that I wasn't locked up with a lunatic, I suffered his pleasantries and light conversation. As the hours went by I warmed to his presence. It seemed he had committed no crime. There was a mix-up with his visa and he had been put in the holding cell until it could be sorted out. It struck me that he might have been terrified to be locked up with a man like me, but he seemed remarkably untroubled.

'You know, you should read this, my brother,' he said, tossing me his book. I read the title, *Through Gates of Splendour*.

'What's it about?' I asked, with disinterest.

'It is a testimony to the marvellous love of the Lord Jesus,' he replied. I politely flicked through the book as he continued to talk. His words reminded me of Martin, the young street preacher and the students I had met in Limassol.

Hours went by and the guards came to release my friend. 'We must stay in touch,' he grinned. 'Come visit me in Lagos.' Writing his name and address in the book, he left it with me and held out his hand. 'God bless you, Tony Anthony,' he said, and he was gone.

The cell had seemed strangely peaceful until then. The Nigerian's chatter had quietened my spirit, but as the night wore on, anger and panic consumed me once more. I had hardened myself towards my parents, but I still felt driven and desperate to find them. I had to get out. As my frenzy rose, the walls started closing in on me. I couldn't get a hold of myself. I gasped for air, feeling as though I was suffocating in my own skin. Beating the bars and screaming to be let out, I threw myself against the walls until I was exhausted.

The floor was damp and dirty and my sweat made tiny puddles in the dust. As I lay there, my eyes picked through a small pile of rubbish under the wooden bench. There was an old and crumpled cola can. Shaking and sweating profusely, I ripped at the half-broken ring pull and began slicing at my wrists. Yelling, cursing and swearing, I scraped at the skin, willing myself to die. The ring pull bent and snapped. With the smaller fragment I tried to run the metal up the main arteries, but to no avail. I was an utter failure. My wrists were bleeding and sore, but I could not inflict a fatal wound. Finally, curling up with my knees to my chest, I fell asleep.

A large, ancient ceiling fan pushed stale air around the musty courtroom. The embassy had arranged some representation for me, but I was in the hands of fast-talking Greeks and I struggled to understand what was going on. No one translated. I felt hopeless, helpless and exhausted with the anger and hatred that had poisoned my soul since Aiya's death. I received a three-year sentence and was too sick and tired to bother caring. An hour later I was on my way to Nicosia Central Prison, the 'fylaki', as I would come to know it. It was Christmas Eve 1989.

A single light bulb cast a greenish hue on badly whitewashed walls. Two officers, both with cigarettes dangling from their mouths, took me through the registration process. I was searched, photographed, fingerprinted and my few belongings were taken away. Handing me a rough blanket, a bar of soap, toilet paper and a small packet of shaving razors, they led me into the depths of the prison. It was an ancient place, with crumbling walls and shafts of light breaking in at random from the low ceiling. We walked down narrow steps and the stench rose up to meet me. Panic was beginning to take hold once again. Digging the remnants of my torn finger nails into my palms, I told myself to stay in control. The guards mumbled to each other and laughed snidely. The stairs opened out into a long corridor of cells. At the end I could see a heavy iron door. Screaming, yelling and hysterical laughter echoed around the stone walls and metal bars. Soon the guards stopped and unlocked a cell door. They gestured towards a lower bunk, whilst babbling instructions at me in Greek.

The place stank of stale sweat and urine. There were seven iron bunk beds secured to the floor by heavy chains. Every imaginable form of human depravity was taking place in that one room. Two men were entwined on one of the top bunks, grunting and moaning together. Below them, a feverish-looking man was pushing a filthy needle into his scab-riddled arm. Another was casually peeling at his skin with a razor blade, chanting to himself and rocking hypnotically. Another was naked, sitting in a pool of urine, cackling to himself.

It was like something out of an X-rated freak show.

Panic seized me. Lunging at the bunk, I yanked the thin flea-ridden mattress off the bed and flung it at the guards. The cell broke into chaos. Men scrambled to get out of my way as I kicked and punched, laying into everyone and everything in an attempt to smash my way out. As one of the guards struggled to pull his truncheon from his belt, I twisted it from his grasp and flung it towards the barred window. It struck one of the men and his blood splattered against the wall. Roaring like a wild animal, I flung myself from bunk to bunk, as screaming, yelling men tried to escape the frenzy.

A stream of guards came rushing in with guns and truncheons. They beat me to the floor and held the weapons tight at my head, shouting at me, 'Hey, fylakis-

menos (prisoner), Stamada! Stamada! Stop!' As I struggled, truncheon blows rained down on me, fast as hail.
They wrestled to pull my arms behind my back and
bound them in a thick leather band. Still I kicked and
writhed until a heavy blow to the back of my head
knocked me out.

Momentarily, I regained consciousness as I felt myself
being half dragged, half carried across cobbled stone. I
was vaguely aware that the air was fresher. We were outside. Every inch of my body throbbed with pain and I
closed my eyes against bright sunlight. My head spun
and I slipped back into unconsciousness.

When I awoke, I was in a tiny concrete room with no
window. It was a freezing cold, vile black hole. In the
dim candlelight, rats and roaches scurried through puddles of stinking human waste. I was lying on a narrow
wooden bench, on which many a desperate soul had
made their mark. A cold sweat broke out over my body
as I carefully felt my wounds. There was no serious damage, but my head throbbed and every muscle ached. It
was deathly quiet. Choking fear gripped me and I felt
like a caged animal. 'Get a grip. Keep hold of yourself,' I
chanted. I tried to meditate, to harness the Ch'i, but the
path towards enlightenment seemed a million light
years away. 'Inner peace.' I had believed it was just
within my reach. Now there was nothing, just a black
hole of terror.

Fearing I was losing my head, I tried to focus mentally on the outside: the jungle-clad slopes of the Hanshan
Si where I had tracked the white tiger; the magnificent
colour of the Cassia and Osmanthus forest, with its
heady scent that drifted through the village in summer-
time; the Swiss Alps where I'd skied; Monaco, where I'd
raced my motorbike, the wind lashing into my sun-
burned face; the boating lake in Hyde Park . . .

Images came flooding into my head, but each beautiful and sensual scene was quickly poisoned: my grandfather's beatings, my parents' abandonment, Aiya in the car . . .

Hours went by and I felt as though I might go crazy. The crumbling walls were ready to suck me up, like an evil predator. I had no idea what time it was or how long I had been there. I shook with cold and terror.

Suddenly, the rumble of a metal trolley made me jump.

A guard smiled at me and something deep within was temporarily rescued. I understood only a little of his Greek, but I welcomed his presence. '*Lamarina*,' he called, handing me a metal plate of boiled eggs, tomatoes, dry bread and hot black tea. I looked at the disgusting mush. 'Eat. Is good for you,' he urged. 'Stay strong.' I took a mouthful of the food and tried to gesture my thanks.

Days went by and I got to know some of the guards, (they were known as '*varianos*', the Turkish word for wardens) who patrolled the block. They seemed to be decent men. I learned that there was another prisoner, a Jew, who was kept in solitary for his own safety. I would come to understand that Nicosia Central Prison was a hive of political hatred and madness. There had been several attempts by the Palestinians and Arabs to kill the Jew. Sometimes, in the dead of night, I thought I heard him singing.

I spent my time staring at the walls and doing a little Tai Chi to keep my body strong. After seven days I was released from solitary confinement and taken back across the cobbled courtyard to a dingy office in the main prison building. A man sat at an antique typewriter, with stacks of files in front of him. He barely looked up as the *varianos* led me in. 'Antonio Anthony,' said one of them in the clerk's direction. The clerk sighed heavily and started burrowing into the records. I stood in silence, wondering what was going to happen next. The two *varianos* perched themselves on a large desk and lit up their cigarettes, all the time chatting to one another as though I wasn't there. Some time passed. Suddenly, the door opened and the *varianos* stood quickly to attention.

A tall, uniformed man entered the room and barked something at them. They immediately stubbed out their cigarettes. A small Turkish-looking character followed hot on the officer's heels. He scurried over to the desk, pulling out the chair ready for his superior to sit down. Next, he dipped into a bag and pulled out a huge cigar and a box of matches. With great care, he placed them down on the desk, then scurried to the corner of the room. There he remained, like a startled rabbit.

Three stripes on his sleeve, and his general air of superiority, told me the uniformed man was a senior-ranking officer. Later, I learned that he was one of a handful of '*chowishis*', who were each in charge of a number of blocks within the massive penitentiary.

The *chowishi* ignored his waiting chair. Instead, he paced the room, circling me, before coming to a standstill, inches in front of my face. I could smell garlic and alcohol on his breath. He looked at me coldly, through deep brown, hawk-like eyes. He said something to the frightened rabbit, who jumped to attention. Taking a file from the clerk, he quickly brought it to the officer, who nonchalantly scanned the notes.

'Ah yez, Mr Anthony. I 'ave 'eard much about you,' he said in heavily-accented English. I didn't know if I should respond, so I remained silent.

'So, you are calmer now, yez?'

I nodded.

'You will go to B-wing. You cause trouble again, you back in solitary. Understand?'

Again, I nodded. That was it. He signalled to the *varianos* and they led me away.

B-wing was just the same as the block I had been taken to on that first day: a long concrete corridor with bars at either end and row upon row of cells. This time I was given a tiny cell to myself. Having seen me smash up thirteen men in the first cell, the authorities obviously believed it was safer that way. It was a squalid hellhole, but I was relieved not to have to share with anyone.

Throughout the day, the cell doors were unlocked and prisoners were able to roam the corridor. Some busied themselves doing arts and crafts, using materials they had bribed the *varianos* for. I quickly learned that everything had a price and both prisoners and guards traded in cigarettes, more serious substances and unsavoury favours. The prisoners were mainly Greeks and Arabs but there were also a few Jews, Germans, a couple of Italians, a Frenchman, a Sri Lankan and an English squaddy named Andy, from Halifax. I intended keeping myself to myself, but as the first few days eked slowly by, I was glad of Andy's friendly banter. He had got into trouble bouncing cheques and was serving a two-year sentence in Nicosia. Foreigners often got unreasonably tough sentences for their crimes. He was a cheery sort, who kept himself clean and fit. He gave me a colourful tour of each cell.

'Murderer, murderer, thief, terrorist, child molester, terrorist, thief, arsonist . . . ' he quickly counted down the cells nearest mine. 'They're all OK,' he said, casually. 'It's the lunatics you gotta watch out for.'

'Lunatics?'

'Yeah mate, the criminally insane. They're a law unto themselves. No reason, y'know,' he said, tapping the side of his head. 'They're unpredictable. Y'never know when they're gonna come at you with a blade.'

Andy's warning didn't trouble me. I knew I could handle myself. What worried me more was seeing the state of some of the men. Some tried to keep their minds and bodies alert, but many were no more than tobacco-puffing living corpses. My mind flashed back to that first cell with the bunk beds. Andy offered me a rancid-looking cigarette. I hesitated then took it. I longed for one of my French Gitanes, but this would do. He continued with the tour. 'It's not like prison back home, mate,' he said. 'Believe me, I know. There's no distinction between crimes in this place. Don't matter whether you're a petty thief, a terrorist or a mass-murdering lunatic. Remember, it's every man for himself here. You gotta watch your back all the time.'

'I'll be OK,' I assured him.

'Yeah, you will. You just gotta follow the rules.'

I couldn't be bothered to ask him whose rules, or what they were. I had my suspicions. Sure enough, I was about to find out.

Every wing had a 'Papas' (often called a 'Mamas' by the other prisoners). I had only been on the block two days before I received a visit. The Papas was an inmate who ruled over the other prisoners and enforced their 'law'. With the exception of the lunatics, who were a law unto themselves, every man was 'owned' by a Papas: his possessions, his earnings, his body. The *varianos* tolerated them, even respected them. It kept some sort of order and they didn't care what went on. I learned that B-wing housed the most notorious and toughest of all the Papas.

'Hello English,' he said as he sauntered, uninvited, into my cell. Four or five of his little minions followed on and lingered at the door. I stood up from the bed. He was a huge, clean-shaven Greek man, with a bulldog face and piggy eyes. 'Welcome to my home,' he said in English, placing his hand warmly on my back. I knew what he was about. 'You are English. I like English,' he said. 'You will be my friend.' His hand moved down below the base of my back.

In an instant, my elbow went straight into his throat. He fell to the floor. The minions fled. *Varianos* poured in from all directions to find the Papas gasping for air. They carried him off to the infirmary. I had probably burst his windpipe. He was never seen on the wing again. I was locked in my cell for the rest of the day. I felt sure there would be further repercussions for me, but nothing happened. Each day went by and I realised word had got around about the new guy who had taken out the Papas. It earned me instant, serious respect that would prove great protection.

For most prisoners every day was a fight for survival, but no one bothered me, except the lunatics who knew no better. I always had to watch my back. The most notorious were Akalias and the one they called 'Alcaponey'. Alcaponey was a huge ogre of a man who picked on other inmates, raping them, cutting, burning or inflicting some other nasty injury, just for pleasure. Akalias was smaller, but just as intimidating. There was something inherently evil about him. He was intelligent and calculating and easily wheedled his way among the *varianos*. Everyone knew he couldn't be trusted. He was an angry, jealous man.

'What's his story?' I asked Andy, one day. 'They say he found his wife in bed with another man,' he said.

'It happens.'

'Yeah, but not every man would have chopped them up. They say he kept pieces of their bodies in his freezer for months.'

'Nasty!'

'Just stay out of his way, man. If he'll let you.'

Unlike Alcaponey, there were times when Akalias could appear to be of reasonably sane mind. Chess was his game. He would force other inmates to play, just for the glory of winning. No one dare beat him. My grandfather had taught me to play chess and in more recent years I had spent many hours with my father who was quite an expert in the game. Akalias was a good match and I enjoyed the challenge. There were times when I felt sure I could beat him, but I had to judge his mood carefully, before taking that gamble. I learned that one time an American man had beaten him and he had chucked hot oil on his face.

Several weeks went by and I got a job with the food trolley, the *Lamarina*, taking it to the hospital and the solitary confinement block. It earned me cigarettes and the opportunity to get out of B-wing for a while. One day as I entered solitary, I thought I heard several voices, laughing and chatting. The *varianos* lazily waved me on towards the cells, in the direction of the noise. I peered into the first cell and saw three men, two Palestinians and one blond-haired white man. '*Lamarina*,' I called. 'Dinner time.'

'Hey, are you English?' asked the blond guy, jumping up.

'Yeah,' I smiled, noting a certain twang that might have been a Geordie accent.

'Ian Davidson,' said the man, offering his hand through the bars.

'Tony,' I said, accepting his firm grasp. The name rang a bell. As if noticing my recognition the man came back, 'Yeah, *that* Ian Davidson. My name's been tabloid fodder for a few years.'

'PLO?'

'Yeah mate, that's it. These are my brothers-in-arms, Elias and Mahmood.' The Palestinians nodded at me.

'A shooting match wasn't it?' I said.

'Yeah,' Ian smiled. 'But don't believe what you read in the papers. The papers had the victims down as tourists, but we'd been watching them for years. They were all Mossad agents. The woman was a notorious car bomber.'

I remembered the story. Ian was from South Shields. The British press had a field day, reporting him as some kind of gun-happy nutcase who joined the Palestinian Liberation Organisation looking for action. He and his friends were arrested during a high profile incident in 1985. They'd been despatched to target two Israeli men and a woman on their yacht in Larnaca Marina. There was a showdown and the group found themselves surrounded by the Cypriot police. Ian and his team knew they could not escape, but by executing the Israelis, they would be imprisoned as heroes. That's exactly what they did to earn their life sentences.

The men had been placed in solitary for their own protection, so the *varianos* were especially lenient. They were allowed to socialise together, to play games, read books and enjoy a few other basic privileges. The guards had even been persuaded to supply them a few seeds so they could grow plants in the tiny secluded courtyard outside the block. That kind of pleasure cannot be underestimated in a hellhole like Nicosia.

Ian was clearly an intelligent man. He'd become involved with the Palestinian cause whilst travelling in America in the 1970s. I couldn't help but admire him and his friends. They were astute, deep-thinking, unexpectedly gentle men, passionate about their cause, for which they were prepared to lay down their lives. Ian also had a wicked sense of humour. I found myself looking forward to the twenty minutes or so each day when I visited them with the *Lamarina*. The *varianos* usually turned a blind eye.

'Word has it we might get out of here in a few days,' Ian told me one day. 'The authorities seem to think the political tension has eased a bit, so they're gonna transfer us to the main block.'

'Do you think there'll be trouble?'

'There'll be a bounty on my head all my life mate, but here, I dunno. There's always the chance Mossad might have someone on the inside, ready to take revenge.'

'It's hard to tell among some of the lunatics,' I laughed.

'Yeah, still, there are a few brothers out there. They seem to know what's going on.'

A few days passed and I was pleased to find that Ian was released onto B-wing. In the months ahead we became good friends. In more recent years, though his whereabouts remain secret, I have kept in touch with Ian since his release from prison. At the time, I never imagined that my friendship with him, and some of the other terrorists, might turn out to be a dangerous liaison.

Chapter 10

Another inmate I grew close to in the early days was Nikos Samson. He spoke good English and had the demeanour of a well-educated man. Like Ian Davidson, he stood out among many of the other *fylakismenos* and I enjoyed his company. Equally, he seemed to warm to me. I could talk politics and current affairs on his level and he played a mean game of *Tavli* (backgammon). A passionate member of the terrorist group EOKA, he fought to unite Cyprus under Greek rule. As the reputed leader of a coup, he briefly ousted the president of Cyprus in 1974. Many of the prisoners and *varianos* still saluted him as the 'eight-day president'. Back in the 50s and 60s he was well known to the British army and police as a feared and ruthless gunman. Now in his 70s, Samson had been in exile in France for many years, but always yearned to return home to his beloved Cyprus. He was arrested as he got off the plane in Larnaca.

Samson was treated like a homecoming war hero. Even in prison, he seemed to want for nothing. As his friend, I could escape the misery of the main block and enjoy the relative luxury of his cell. It had been decorated with paintings and beautiful artwork and there was a television, radio and a couple of easy chairs. It was almost surreal to think this room was only a little way from my own pit of a cell. There was no shortage of chocolate or fruit and even the occasional bottle of brandy. Knowing my preference for French cigarettes, Samson procured a steady supply of Gitanes.

I remained careful, however. It is easy for a man to become 'owned' in that kind of situation. I repaid him for the cigarettes with my sketches and paintings. That was how I 'earned' my 'livelihood', painting portraits from people's photographs, or writing calligraphy nameplates. With Samson's help, I was never short of materials. But I was also very wary of his racial standing. He must have known I had a British passport, but he never hid his hatred towards the English.

'See this?' he asked me, lifting up his shirt to reveal deep scars. 'The Brits. Thank you Her Majesty! Talk about the British secret service. They have no idea.'

'What. They tortured you?'

'How else do you think I got these? Still, they got nothing out of me,' he said with a wry smile.

Samson was a good person to know but, as time went by, I began to realise what he was up to. I quickly ended my association with him.

Some nights word got around that no one was to go near Samson's side of the wing. It was an unwritten rule, but even the officers enforced it. Only certain inmates were allowed to visit him at these times. They were the vulnerable type.

One cold night a group of us huddled around the stove, clinging to every last ember of warmth, before the *varianos* caged us in our icy cells. The cold was the prison's natural torture mechanism. Day after day I woke up shivering, breathing cloudy vapour into the air. It was impossible to warm up all day. Even if you remained active, your hands and feet felt like permanent blocks of ice. The thought of another long night ahead was enough to freeze the mind as well as the body.

Spying Panayiotos, nervously shivering in the darkness, I called him over. He was a young, good-looking Greek lad serving a short sentence for petty theft. He couldn't handle prison and I generally tried to keep an eye out for him. I was hardly the compassionate type, but it wasn't right the way some of the weaker prisoners got taken advantage of. There were knowing whispers among the other men, as Panayiotos shuffled over from the direction of Samson's cell. 'Come and join us,' I said again. 'The fire's almost dead, but it's better than nothing.' Without looking at anyone, Panayiotos pulled up a stool. He clasped his hands tightly together. He was trembling and I realised it was more than the cold that was getting to him.

'What is it, Panayiotos?' I asked, in Greek. He silently stared into the dying flames.

In the weeks ahead, Panayiotos retreated more into his pale, tortured stare. His eyes were permanently swollen and he couldn't look me in the face when I tried to talk to him. Every evening, at a particular time, Panayiotos visited Samson's cell. He had become his slave. There were nasty rumours about the goings on. The *varianos* let it slip about the number of used condoms they cleared from Samson's cell. I usually had no time for prison gossip but, though Samson never made any such advance towards me, I'd had my own suspicions for a while. Samson was soon to be released and word had it that he'd set up a job for his new young friend, 'working' for him on the outside.

It sickened me to the core every time I looked at Panayiotos' haunted face. Sometimes I felt almost overwhelmed with rage and disgust. But Samson wasn't a man to tackle. Even I knew that.

Despite the friendships I made and the camaraderie between the English-speaking inmates, prison was doing little to curb my aggression. Winter was painful, but short. Summer seemed to come quickly. Within days the stifling heat in the prison was as torturous as winter's chill. Whilst the cold had made the prisoners lethargic and lazy, the heat just seemed to fuel the torment. Tempers ran high and there were daily skirmishes.

Sometimes a fight would start over nothing and quickly escalate to all-out war. Perhaps someone had sat on the wrong stool, or said the wrong thing to the wrong person. It took nothing. Other fights were politically motivated, usually between Greeks and Arabs, but we all joined in. I loved it. It gave me something to do. One day there had been an electric atmosphere on the block since early rising. By mid-morning exercise, the murmurings and usual racial taunts had turned into loud abuse. All of a sudden, an Arab ringleader took a swing at one of the Greeks. The battle began. Clouds of dust were kicked up in the courtyard and blood splattered the cobblestones as flesh and concrete compounded. Adrenaline flooded my veins.

It wasn't my war, but I was more than happy to fight. I didn't care who I hit, I just lashed out. One of the maniacs came flying at me from behind, trying to take a punch at the back of my head. I spun around to see him towering above me, laughing, about to deliver another blow. I launched a stop punch to his nose, bludgeoning him against a wall whilst his blood splashed back at my face. He was a huge brute. He came straight back at me. I curved my body to absorb his incoming blow to my stomach and jabbed my tiger claws into his eyes. The fighting went on and on. All manner of weapons appeared from nowhere: blades, knives, truncheons. Suddenly, there was gunfire. The army had arrived. They rounded us up and carted broken bodies off to the infirmary. The rest of us were locked in our cells early that day.

One day, soon after that, Andy joined me over breakfast. The place was really beginning to get to me and he probably knew it. 'You never have any visitors do you, Tony?' I looked up from the slop of my porridge. 'That's cos there ain't no one, mate,' I said, smiling weakly. 'What about you?

'There's this guy called Michael Wright . . . '

'Michael Wright?' I interrupted. 'I know that name. Is he Irish?'

'Yeah, from Belfast. He's with some kind of church. Bit of a do-gooder, y'know the sort.' I snorted in agreement, as Andy continued. 'I tell you man, when you ain't got no one else, it's good just to see anybody from the outside.' We sat in silence for a while.

'I told him about you,' Andy said tentatively. 'He said he'd like to meet you.' I was a little taken aback. Why would he be interested in me? I wondered. 'Naw,' I said. 'I don't think I need anyone. Thanks anyway, mate.' We changed the subject.

A few days later I received a letter. It was the first time there had been any mail for me. At first, my heart leapt, but I soon noted the writing on the envelope was not that of my mother or father. Curious, I tore it open. It turned out to be from this guy, Michael Wright. It was a nice letter, fluent and friendly. I poured over the words again and again, like a man hungry for communication. Its message was straightforward. Michael made no attempt to hide his agenda. He simply told me that he would like to meet me, to visit me as a friend, because of the love of Jesus. I laughed. What a strange thing to say. Still, I was intrigued. What harm could it do to meet him? If he could be bothered to come into this stinking hole, the least I could do was accept his visit, just once. If nothing else, it would get me a half hour change of scene and possibly even a Mars bar or a drink from the visitors' canteen.

I sent Michael a visiting order. Thursday came and a *variano* led me up to the visitors' room to meet him. The room still had the same musty smell of decay that spewed out from all areas of the prison, but the air was fresher here and sunshine streamed in through the windows. I was surprised to feel nervous at the thought of meeting someone. The *variano* gestured to the long narrow wooden table. Guests sat on one side, inmates on the other. Michael hadn't yet arrived. The room was full of noisy Greeks with their visiting wives, children, girl-friends, mothers and fathers. It was strange to see ordinary people again. I felt I had no place there.

Suddenly, I was painfully aware of my dishevelled appearance and felt as though I wore my crimes on my sleeve. What did this God-fearing man want with me? I grew more nervous and uncomfortable but, just when I thought I might get up and head back to the prisoners' entrance; a tall, bearded man was shown into the room and escorted towards me. 'What an idiot,' I thought, seeing his beaming smile. He wore nylon slacks and a crumpled shirt, with sleeves slightly too short. 'Tony,' he said in his Northern Irish accent, still beaming and holding out his hand. 'It's wonderful to see you. Thank you for allowing me to meet you. I've heard so much about you.' I was instantly on guard, but held out my hand. He grasped it in both his, and shook it warmly. That unnerved me all the more. I began to feel my usual anger rising up inside.

Michael sat down opposite me, still smiling. He obviously saw my anguish. 'Tony, I'm here as a friend,' he said. 'I'm not here to preach at you . . . ' I looked at him scornfully. 'I'm here because of the love of Jesus Christ,' he continued. 'Everyone at our church is praying for you and we want to support you as much as we can.' No one had talked to me this way before. I didn't know what to say, but I couldn't let myself trust him. Fury was begin-ning to take hold. We sat quietly for a while, my mind whirling. What was it with this guy?

At the table next to us a young Greek was saying goodbye to his parents. His mother broke into tears as they embraced and was led away sobbing. My parents would never visit me in this hellhole. Did they even know I was here? My thoughts came fast and furious, but I was aware that Michael was still talking. At least he'd bothered to turn up. Perhaps I would play along with him for a while. If he annoyed me too much I could easily grab him, pull him over the table and beat his head in.

I listened to Michael's chatter, not caring to say much or even meet his gaze. 'Tony, I would like to come and see you again. Next week, maybe. What do you think?' I had no idea what I thought, but gave a slight nod. 'God bless you, Tony. I will look forward to seeing you soon.' I watched him leave.

'Idiot,' I thought, cursing under my breath.

The next Thursday, however, I agreed to see Michael again. By the third and fourth week I found I was looking forward to seeing that stupid smile. He was my window to the outside world. He talked to me of everyday things: eating watermelon in the cool of the evening, a Dairy Queen burger bar opening up in Nicosia . . . 'Oh, for a burger. It's been too long,' I smiled.

'It's the Greek coffee I struggle with,' he laughed. 'It turns my head thick! I'm visiting a lot of the little village coffee shops, "*kafeneions*" they call them, don't they?'

I nodded, smiling at his attempt at Greek pronunciation.

'The old guys there are usually very welcoming. I've been taking them "Good Seed" calendars.' He pulled one out of his pocket. 'See, they're just inspirational pictures, with a Bible passage for each day.' He read a couple to me.

Through Michael's news and stories I could remember what it was like to be free. 'Freedom' was something he sometimes mentioned, but it was nothing to do with prisons or cells. He talked about 'freedom in Christ'. I didn't ask him about it and he stuck to his promise not to preach. He would just naturally drop things into his conversation about what 'the Lord' had been doing in his life that week. He told me what was going on at his church and enthused about the youth camps he was running in the Troodos Mountains. I tolerated his casual church talk. I liked to hear about other people's lives. He helped me keep a grip on reality.

Michael's support involved more than just visiting. He wrote every week and also sent letters from other people in his church. I devoured them. He began sending books. It didn't matter what they were about, I just feasted on the words. Most of the other books and magazines, left lying around by the prisoners, were pornographic. I longed for something, anything, of substance.

Michael came to see me almost every Thursday for the next six months. He always prayed before he left. 'Silly fool,' I thought, 'smiling there with his eyes closed, talking into space as though God could really hear him.'

There were a couple of occasions when he was unable to visit, but he sent others in his place. A dear old lady called Valerie showed up. I admired her bravery, coming into a place like this, but she had the same warmth as Michael and I enjoyed her gentle chatter. Another time there was Richard Knox. Richard had already written a couple of letters to me. He had been a missionary in Beirut, Lebanon for many years and we shared some common ground talking about our experiences in the Middle East. His stories were quite different from the recollections of my time there with the close protection unit, but I respected his guts. It wasn't an easy place to live, especially with a wife and family. Like Michael, he had a passion to help people, just because of, as they said, the 'love of Jesus Christ'.

I was barely conscious of it at the time, but Michael and his friends were somehow beginning to reach me. They were very different from anyone else I'd ever met. They had this strange interest in me that I really didn't understand. It amazed me that total strangers could show such friendship to someone who clearly didn't deserve it. I really looked forward to seeing them or receiving their letters.

Still, six months in the *fylaki* does things to your mind. All my life I had learned to trust no one and to be constantly on my guard. I didn't like the way I was becoming dependent on my new friends. The more I thought about it, the more paranoid I became. One Thursday morning, 3 May 1990, I lay on my bunk thinking about Michael. I had woken up feeling angry, with him on my mind. What was he up to? What did he really want with me? The books he'd sent me were in a neat pile on the floor. Recently, he'd sent me a Bible, but I couldn't be bothered with it. I read a few bits at the beginning and soon lost interest. He was trying to brainwash me. That was it. He wanted to recruit me into his weird cult. How dare he play with me like this? How dare he talk of freedom and tease me with his stories from the outside? I thought back to the way his name had cropped up the week before my arrest. Then, here he was, laughing at me in prison. Just who was he? I'd have him for it. No more messing about.

It was straight in my mind. That afternoon I would confront him. If he didn't tell me what he was really up to, I'd smash his face in.

By the time I got to the visitors' room later that afternoon, fury was really beginning to boil within me.

Sitting at the table, waiting for Michael, I was seething with anger. The mêlée of visiting Greek families usually irritated or upset me, but today I focused only on my animosity towards Michael. Where was he? He was late. He was playing with me, even now.

The door opened and Michael entered with his usual ear-to-ear stupid grin. I felt like a coiled snake, waiting for my prey. I cursed him under my breath. Pulling up a chair he could not help but notice the tension. He was immediately serious. 'What's wrong Tony? What's happened?' he asked anxiously.

'Why are you coming here Michael?' I asked, aggressively. 'What do you really want from me?' Michael sat back in his chair and looked at me calmly. I wanted to smash him there and then.

'Tony, I'm coming to see you because of Jesus.' He paused. I could easily reach him and yank him across the table.

'Jesus loves you, Tony.'

I swore to myself. Michael wasn't deterred.

'I believe God wants to communicate with you through me.'

Here we go, I thought. This is the brainwashing stuff.

'I'm here just to show you his love.' Michael continued to look at me, straight in the face.

'Jesus can set you free from the prison you're in,' he said. That really upset me. How dare he talk about freedom with me behind bars? It was OK for him; he could get up and walk away any time he liked.

'Go on then, Michael,' I snarled. 'Tell me how Jesus can get me out of here. How do you reckon he's gonna set me free? How can you talk about Jesus like he really exists? Have you ever met this Jesus, have you seen him?' I fired the questions at him in arrogance and rude contempt, but Michael didn't waver. He had no fear.

Why wasn't he backtracking, trying to get away from me? Why wasn't he scared of me? He knew I could easily hurt him. Instead, Michael set about answering my questions. I couldn't smash him. Not yet.

'Yes, Tony,' he said, with deep conviction. 'Yes, I've met Jesus.' I frowned at him in disbelief, but he continued. 'My parents showed me the truth about Jesus Christ from an early age, Tony,' he said. 'I went along to their church youth club and learned more about this man Jesus, the Son of God.' He continued, 'It tells us in the Bible, " . . . if you confess with your mouth, 'Jesus is Lord,' and believe in your heart that God raised him from the dead, you will be saved." That's what I did. I believed that Jesus paid a great price for me.'

'What price?' I interrupted, savagely.

'I was a sinner. I deserved to die, but when Jesus chose to die on the cross, he took my place and paid for my sins with his own blood, so that I could know the love of God and be forgiven.'

I laughed mockingly at him. 'What? You were a child. How could you think you deserved to die? I bet you'd never even done anything wrong.'

Michael came back at me. 'It says in the Bible that no one is perfect. We are all sinners, Tony. We have the freedom to choose between right and wrong and, even as small children, we move away from God's perfect will. You know you do things that are wrong. I know I do things that are wrong . . . '

'Yeah, so what's your point? Come on Michael, spit it out,' I said rudely. He sat forward in his chair.

'God made us, Tony. He made the universe and everything in it. He is the true Father. But he is a perfect God and he cannot look at us because we are so full of sin, of wrongdoing. Because of this, we are separated from him.'

I glared at Michael angrily, but it didn't put him off. 'I came to understand, when I was just a young boy, that God still loves us, like a father. He wants a relationship with us, even with all our wickedness and wrongdoing. That's why he had to send his son to earth, to live among us and die in our place. Jesus was God, becoming man.'

Michael's talk of a loving father angered me all the more. It made me think again of the way my parents had abandoned me. Michael seemed to read my mind.

'Tony, people will always let you down. Your parents let you down. Friends let you down. I will let you down. What if I don't show up for visiting next week when you're expecting me? It might be through no fault of my own. I might get stuck in traffic. But I will still have let you down.'

'So?'

'So, God will not do that to you. He loves you so very much. God promises in the Bible that he will never leave you, nor forsake you.'

That silenced me for a moment. I bit hard into my lip. I was beginning to tremble with rage.

'OK Michael, so if he exists and he loves me so much, where is he now? Why doesn't he help me while I'm stuck in this shit-hole?'

'God has been visiting you for a long time, Tony, through me, through Valerie and Richard, through others you've met. He is trying to tell you how much he wants you to know him. Listen, it tells us in the Bible, in the Gospel of John, chapter 3, verse 16: "For God so loved the world that he gave his one and only Son, that whoever believes in him shall not perish but have eternal life."' Michael stopped again, letting the words hang in the air.

'Eternal life? What the hell would I want with that, Michael? I hate my life.'

'You hate your life because you're a prisoner, you're not free,' he replied. There he was, off again, about freedom. Still, I had to give him credit; he was not giving up on me.

'But that doesn't answer my question, Michael,' I spat. 'If this wonderful God loves me so much, why doesn't he just appear? Why does he have to hide himself in you, or Richard, or Valerie? Is he chicken?' I thought it was a smart enough question. Michael sat back and thought for a while. 'Ha! Gotcha.'

Then he spoke, with calmness and authority. 'Tony, if God appeared now in this room, you would be flat on the floor on your face. You would be absolutely terrified. You could not even attempt to look into his glorious face. And that's exactly why he sent Jesus, so that through him you can come before God and know his love,' Michael finished.

I didn't even try to digest what he was telling me. I was still trying to provoke him. 'I've managed quite well without your God all my life. What makes you think I need him now, eh? Come on Michael, answer me this!' I slammed my fist down on the table. A *variano* jumped to attention, but Michael held his hand up to him reassuringly. He never took his eyes from mine.

'All your life, you've had a God-shaped hole in your heart that you've been trying to fill,' Michael started. 'You've tried to fill it with Kung Fu, Buddhism; you've tried the glory of being a winner and being the best at your work; you've tried sex, drugs, anger, violence . . . None of these things have given you the satisfaction you crave. The one thing you have not tried is Jesus Christ.' Now he slapped his hand down on the table. Michael was passionate and animated. He held up a bunch of keys. 'Tony, imagine for a minute these keys are the keys to your cell. Imagine I gave them to you and tonight all the guards fell asleep and you were able to let yourself out.'

Now he was getting closer to a slapping. What kind of rubbish was this?

Michael continued, 'Imagine you climbed over the prison wall and got out into the Turkish sector and got away.' He looked at me intently. 'Would you be free?' he asked.

'What sort of stupid question is this?' I demanded. 'Of course I would be free. What are you talking about?'

'No, Tony, you would not be free.' He was smiling now. 'You wouldn't be free, because you would still be the same Tony. You may change your haircut, your clothes, the amount of money in your pocket, where you live. You may change many things about yourself, but you will always be Tony. You will always make the same mistakes that you've made all your life. You'll never be able to wipe the slate clean of your past. You'll always get angry. You may calm down a bit, but if I press this button, or that button, you'll still flip. That's because you haven't fitted Jesus into that huge hole in your heart. You are not satisfied with your life. You never will be without him.'

I tried to butt in with something stupid, but Michael continued, 'You might get out of here and earn a lot of money, have a big house and a car, a family even, but I promise, Tony, you will still be the same. These things will not bring you what you are really looking for. And what if your life was taken from you today? Money can do nothing for you. Neither can family or friends, or any of the things you gather around yourself. None of these things can set you free.' Sweat was beginning to form on his brow. He went on, 'These things are like drugs, they give you a temporary high, make you feel like you're happy for a while, but none of them can set you free, none of them can bring you satisfaction. Tony, listen to me,' he paused and drew breath. 'The Bible says, "If the Son (of God) sets you free, you shall be free indeed."'

That phrase seemed to linger in my head. 'You shall be free indeed.' I felt goose bumps rise on my arms.

The bell rang to signal the last five minutes of visiting. Michael was getting through to me, but I was still angry and wanted to show him so. I still thought I might hit him, but he was putting up a good argument. He leaned forward, looking up at me through piercing eyes. 'Whoever believes in him, Tony. That's all you have to do. Jesus has already done the work. He has already made the way so that you can turn from your wrongdoing, you can be forgiven. It's not about religious practices or becoming a "goody two shoes". It's about trusting in God's work of salvation. All you have to do is believe and accept his free gift.'

My mind flicked back to the night in Limassol when I had watched the young street preacher with his bottle of wine.

'Tony, you've talked to me before about following the way of Kung Fu, but let me tell you, Jesus Christ said, "I am the way and the truth and the life. No-one comes to the Father except through me." Kung Fu might claim to be *a* way, but he is *the* way. Just accept it, Tony.'

Now he had me. He was speaking my language. I looked down at the table. I was quieter now.

'You have no idea what I'm like. The things I've done. How could anyone ever help me?' I said, fighting something that was going on in my spirit. Michael came back again, quoting from the Bible.

'In Romans 8 verse 1, we are told, "Therefore, there is now no condemnation for those who are in Christ Jesus, because through Christ Jesus the law of the Spirit of life set me free from the law of sin and death."'

I looked up at Michael. He saw that I was struggling to take in what he'd said.

'No condemnation, Tony. The slate is wiped clean. You start again. Jesus takes your sin and destroys it. These words were written by the apostle Paul.'

Michael began to explain. 'He was an evil murderer who persecuted Christians. But, this is what I'm trying to say to you. *No one* is beyond the love of God, Tony. Paul, in the worst of his sin, met with the Lord Jesus and was transformed by him. He went on to bring thousands of others into that same life-saving relationship with God. Jesus was working in him, despite the terrible deeds of his past and his continuing human failings. You see, Tony, God is a God of second chances.'

Michael had addressed my deepest fear. In the last few months I had begun to think that my life was truly worthless that, in prison, I was getting exactly what I deserved and that nothing or no one could help me. I believed I was unreachable, but Michael went on to talk to me about other people in the Bible who God had transformed.

'Remember when I first came in today I talked about how everyone makes mistakes, everyone is a sinner?' he said. 'Everyone needs forgiveness. Through Jesus, that is freely given. All we have to do is ask.' Michael was talking quickly now, quoting more scripture.

'Romans chapter 3, verse 22: "This righteousness from God comes through faith in Jesus Christ to all who believe. There is no difference, for all have sinned and fall short of the glory of God, and are justified freely by his grace through the redemption that came by Christ Jesus."' Again I tried to grapple with Michael's words.

I was still agitated, but the words, 'You shall be free indeed,' were ringing in my head. Michael leaned closer, until he was almost lying on the table.

'You can choose to accept Jesus into your heart any time you like, Tony,' he said. 'But remember, you don't know when your life will be demanded of you. The Bible says, "today" is the day of salvation, so don't delay.'

I avoided his eye contact. 'So how?' I asked quietly.

'You need to pray to God and ask him to forgive you. Tell him you want to receive Jesus as your saviour. Tell him you want to believe in him and put your trust in him, even though you can't see him. Thank Jesus that he died for you on the cross, so that you can receive God's love.'

The bell rang signalling the end of visiting.

'Is that it?' I asked, cynically.

'That's it, but if you say that prayer, Tony, you have to mean it. You have to turn away from your old life, stop doing the wrong things you do. It won't be easy, but Jesus will help you.'

The room was beginning to empty. Michael closed his eyes to pray. 'Lord Jesus, we thank you that you are here with us in this prison. Thank you for the work you are doing in Tony's life. Thank you that you love Tony so much. I pray, Father, that Tony will soon accept your love. Amen.'

I did not look up from the table. 'I will see you next week, my friend,' said Michael. I dug my fingers into my palms and said nothing.

Chapter 11

I made my way quickly back along B-wing, my mind whirling with Michael's words. The heat, stench and general misery of the place was more oppressive than ever. The walls seemed to be closing in on me. I was a caged animal, vicious, but terrified. One of the maniacs was loitering outside my cell, dragging on a cigarette and laughing to himself as he blew the smoke out through his nose. As I pushed past him, he stabbed the cigarette into my right arm, leaving an instant and nasty burn. He'd picked a bad day to wrong me. The full weight of my fury rained down on him. I grabbed him by the hair and smashed his face into the wall, continuing to push and scrape his head against the harsh, jagged stone until blood spurted over us both. By the time I'd finished, he was unrecognisable and his nose was virtually hanging off his face.

Back in my cell I was a tormented soul. Michael's words wouldn't leave me. I screwed my eyes shut and covered my ears, trying to rid myself of them. But there they were, over and over. And there was Michael's smile and those piercing eyes that wouldn't let me go. Why was I so important to him? I began to think about who I was and what I'd become. All my life I'd needed no one. I was strong and successful and in control. But Michael had talked about 'fullness of life' and 'joy in abundance'. Certainly in these months in prison there had been no satisfaction in my life. I thought about my Kung Fu, winning competitions and about my work in close protection security. Perhaps Michael was right. I'd enjoyed the money, the fast living and the adrenaline highs, but it was never enough. I always wanted to be better, to have more. Now all that had been taken away from me and my art wasn't what it used to be. Even at the busiest of times, I'd always maintained a daily training schedule, exercising for a minimum of five hours. These days, I had all the time in the world, but it didn't matter any more. I couldn't be bothered. As for meditation and the search for enlightenment, that required a peaceful and disciplined mind. My head was full of violence, of the hour-by-hour fight for survival. I had become like the rest of the animals in there, messing around with their drugs and involving myself in their futile feuds, just to pass the time. 'Fullness of life', what did that mean? The only time I'd felt anything close to that was in those years with Aiya.

Now I was on dangerous ground. In the past few months I'd not allowed myself to think about her. I recalled her beautiful innocent face and began to tremble. Yes, she had taught me what love could be, but now she was gone. I closed my eyes and remembered how she lovingly fingered my face, seeing me in her blindness. Suddenly my mind was filled with the image of the maniac outside my cell and the way I had destroyed him. I imagined Aiya 'seeing' him, tracing the broken bones and split skin, feeling the stickiness of his blood. In my head she screamed. She had loved me, but would she love me now, if she knew what I had become? No way! How could she love me when I had beaten a man half to death and maimed him for life?

I buried my head in the mattress and pulled the pillow round my ears, trying to force the images away. My whole body was racked with terror.

'God loves you so much, Tony'.

They were Michael's words. They ran over and over in my head and there was nothing I could do to shut them out. I fought with them, but as the minutes ticked by the words seemed to be calming me. I tried to remember the verse that Michael talked about. It came to me, in bits and pieces. 'God so loved the world that he gave his son . . . ' Understanding somehow came to me. God has already 'given'. Jesus has already died and nothing I had done in the past or will do in the future will change that. I thought again about the man outside. Surely God could not tolerate this, surely I needed to be punished? ' . . . whoever believes in him will not perish, but will have life.' Again, I thought about each word as I tried to piece the passage together from memory. The sentences seemed to be coming into my head, as though someone was right there in the room, reciting them for me, willing me to understand. 'Whoever believes . . . whoever believes.' Mulling over the words, I came to a strange realisation. The ball was firmly in my court. If I was to go any further with this, I had to believe what Michael had been telling me about Jesus.

Where do I start? Again the image of the broken man haunted me. I let out a cry. 'Sorry, oh my God, I'm sorry!'

The floodgates came crashing down.

Images of my life flashed before me like a movie. It was as though I was free-falling through a torturous tunnel of anguish. In mental agony, my mind's eye fell upon broken and maimed bodies, lives I had ruined, terror I'd inflicted. 'Please God, if you're there, forgive me,' I cried. The movie ran faster. I tried to slow it down, to remember everything, but in my torment I was saying sorry to God, even for things I could not recall. I was wailing and gasping for air. I could barely swallow and was aware that my cries were becoming louder and more frenzied.

I stuffed the pillow into my face for fear of the other men hearing me. Still I went on and on, laying myself bare before God. Hours must have gone by.

When I finally got up, my cell was in darkness. The door had been locked and the prison was quiet. Looking up through the tiny window I could see the moon. My eyes focused on the bars and picked up the light shining on their intersection. I looked on the cross of Calvary, the cross on which Jesus died. I didn't need to recall Michael's words. They came flooding back to me. I prayed, asking Jesus for forgiveness, asking him to fill that hole in my life, promising that I would turn away from my old life and start again with him. I talked to Jesus all night, until finally I fell asleep.

The next morning everything seemed different. For as long as I could remember I had been angry. Now that feeling had gone. I was calm, peaceful somehow. I sat up in bed, looking at the little square of sunlight beyond the bars. It was a beautiful day outside. I realised that in the last few months I had rarely even looked out of the window. I hadn't cared to torment myself with thoughts of what I was missing. I felt a strange warmth, even though the sun had yet to heat the thick stone walls of the prison block. Remembering the previous day, and the outpouring of the night, I smiled and whispered, 'Thank you Jesus.' I didn't begin to understand what had happened to me, but I knew something had changed. I felt like a huge weight had been lifted from me. I wanted to talk to Michael and decided to write a letter telling him I had prayed and that I knew Jesus had saved me. He would be excited.

The sound of my cell door being unlocked startled me. The prison was coming to life and there was the usual shouting and general noise of men pouring out onto main corridor. Suddenly, I was aware that I was ravenously hungry. I never had any appetite for the prison slop, but now I looked forward to my lukewarm bowl of porridge. Leaping up from my bed I caught sight of my cigarettes and realised that, although I'd been awake for over an hour, I'd not even thought about lighting up. Usually, I couldn't leave my bed until I'd had at least a couple of fags. Smiling in amazement, I picked up the packet and threw them out of sight, under the bed.

A large redheaded brute stood in front of my door. He was one of the madmen and my mind flashed back to the previous evening. There was still blood on the floor. I cringed at the memory and tried to ease myself past the redhead. He spun round, swearing as he touched his cigarette down on my left arm. I looked him straight in the face, brushed the ash from my flesh and walked away. As I reached the breakfast area I could not believe what had happened. I examined my arm where the burn should have been. There was nothing there. My arms were covered in scars from previous such incidents and the burn from last night was still sore, but there was nothing new, not a single mark.

A few days later I was sitting in the library writing another letter to Michael. I had many questions for him and was even more hungry for his communication. Shane, a young Sri Lankan man, was sitting close by, doing some artwork. The place could hardly be called a library. It was another dungeon-type room, with a few tattered books scattered on makeshift tables. Still, it was peaceful and I had been spending a lot of time there recently, away from the continual screaming and fighting on the main block. As I scribbled, my heart was bursting with joy. Despite the squalid surroundings, I felt that life couldn't have been any better.

Shane had managed to get hold of a flask of hot water and some heavily recycled dregs of coffee. He handed me a tin cup.

'What's with you, Tony?' he asked. 'You've got a stupid grin on your face and you look as though you're about to dance around the room at any minute.' I laughed aloud. 'Come on man, what are you taking. Cut me in on some,' the Sri Lankan said.

'I'm not taking anything, Shane,' I said, still laughing. He came up close and looked into my eyes. He was serving time for drug smuggling and knew all the signs of a user.

'You're taking something, otherwise why would you be so happy?' he asked suspiciously.

I certainly felt high, but it had nothing to do with any chemical. 'I'm just happy, Shane, I've got Jesus in my life.' There, I'd said it.

'Ah, "Jesus", that's a new one on me. Haven't heard it called that before. Where'd ya get it?' Shane asked.

'No, man, I'm serious. The other night I prayed to God and I'm a changed man. I'm just so happy.'

Now Shane was laughing, too. He clearly didn't believe what I was saying, but I went on to tell him about Michael, about his visits and the things he had told me about Jesus.

'I don't need drugs to feel this good, Shane. Listen to me; you know what I'm talking about? Each time you take a hit, you feel good. But then you need more and more to keep feeling that way. That's not happiness, Shane, it's addiction. It wheedles away at you until it's got you firmly in its grasp then, when you're at your most desperate, it wastes you away to nothing.' Shane nodded, knowingly.

I told Shane about my prayer and about my anger disappearing. I told him about the cigarette burns and other astonishing things that had happened since that night when I gave my life to Jesus.

'I've noticed a change in you,' he said. 'I just thought you'd got some good stuff.' He was shaking his head in amazement. I recalled the words from John 3:16, saying to him, 'All you have to do is say a prayer and believe it.'

Shane searched my face. He knew what I was saying was true. He asked questions, but he didn't argue with me, the way I had with Michael. 'What I don't get, though, is why Jesus had to die. Why did God want him to do that?' he asked. I thought for a few moments. It was all very new to me, too. Now I believed. I'd experienced God and his amazing gift of forgiveness through Jesus myself, but explaining it to someone else – especially someone whose first language wasn't English – was quite a challenge.

'God is a perfect God, Shane,' I began. 'We are not perfect. We are all sinners. Even the most good-living person in the world has still fallen short of God's standard. It tells us this in the Bible. But that doesn't mean God doesn't love us. In truth, he longs for us to be with him. When he sent his son, Jesus, to earth it was because he wanted, in the only way he could, to become fully human for a time. That was his way of showing us that he really does understand what it's like to live on the earth and to struggle the way we do.'

'Yeah, OK, go on,' said Shane eagerly.

'So, when Jesus died, he died in our place. He took on all our sin, so that we could be forgiven and made perfect before God. That's why Jesus was the perfect sacrifice. He took the death that we deserve, so we don't have to. We can choose life.'

'So, it's like we all need to be punished because of the wrong things we've done, but God has let us off?'

'Yeah, well, nearly. It's not just that God has let us off. A sentence still needs to be served for our wrong. That's what Jesus did.' I thought for a while then tried to explain it more clearly in a story. 'There were two boys who grew up together as best friends. As the years went by they went their separate ways. One had a good career and became a judge. The other fell on hard times, got mixed up with the wrong company and became a thief. One day the judge realised that the man standing in the dock before him was none other than his old childhood friend who he had loved dearly. He had an awful dilemma. As a judge, he was bound to uphold the law. He knew that he had to serve the thief with a large fine. He also knew that his friend could not pay. If he didn't pay, he would be condemned to prison.'

'So what happened? asked Shane.

'Well, the judge passed sentence, as he was bound to. But then he stood down and took off his judge's wig and his gown. To the utter amazement of everyone else in the courtroom he joined his old friend in the dock, took out his chequebook and paid the fine on behalf of the man he loved. His friend was free to go. No fine, no prison sentence, no debt at all.'

'So the judge represents Jesus, right?

'Yeah, well, he represents God. Remember, he was bound by the law, because he was the law. He couldn't just decide to ignore his friend's wrongdoing. Instead, he had to pay for it himself. He couldn't do that as the judge. That's why, for a time, he took off his judges garments and placed himself in the dock, alongside the thief.'

'Right, now I get it. Tell me that verse again. The one about believing and getting life . . . '

'It's from the Gospel of John, chapter 3, verse 16: "For God so loved the world that he gave his one and only Son, that whoever believes in him shall not perish but have eternal life."' As I spoke, tears began to prick in Shane's eyes.

'Do you want to do it?' I urged. 'Do you want to find forgiveness and peace and joy with God, the way I have?'

'Yes,' said Shane, with urgency. 'But I don't know what to say, I don't know how to pray.'

'I'd never prayed either, before the other night,' I reminded him. 'We can do it together if you want.' I led him through the words. He repeated them after me, asking God to forgive him, telling him that he wanted to turn away from his old life and let Jesus into his heart. It was the first time I'd ever prayed with or for anyone. It felt good. Tears ran down Shane's face and he grasped my hands in his, now praying his own prayer, letting the words fall out in his own language. I didn't understand a word he was saying, but I knew it was a heartfelt prayer.

I arranged for Michael to visit Shane and he provided us both with Emmaus Bible study courses. Shane spoke reasonably good English but Michael and I were desperate that he should have a Sri Lankan Bible. There was little I could do from inside the prison, except pray. In the meantime, Michael put word out among his church. Remarkably, a lady came forward, saying she had found a Sri Lankan Bible in her house. Shane was overjoyed. Within a few weeks he was miraculously clean of his long-term drug addiction.

It wasn't long before Michael was on the hunt for a German Bible. Ziggy – Zeigfried Von Greber, as he first introduced himself – was a chain-smoking hulk of a man in his late 40s, from Berlin. A wheeler-dealer, he looked like a hell's angel, with long grey-blond hair, an unkempt wiry moustache and a big belly that poked out from under his T-shirt. He was cocky and arrogant – a rebel without a cause, who worked the system, any system, just for the sake of it. He always managed to get extra food from the kitchen. He was serving time for smuggling and told a good story, though I doubted that much of what he said was true. There was the European connection between us and from my early days in the prison we got on OK. He was a creative man who spent his time making intricate models of boats from matchsticks. We cooked up deals together, whiling away the hours with my painting and his model making: our work was good currency and we were rarely short of cigarettes or other extras.

He laughed when I first told him about my meeting with Jesus and took to calling me 'preacher'. He respected me, but like many other men inside, the world had corrupted him and he had no time for religion. I knew that he had no one to visit him, so after several weeks of cajoling, I persuaded him to send a visiting order for Michael Wright. He seemed to enjoy the visits, but when he started to abuse Michael behind his back, I soon realised that they were just another of Ziggy's schemes. Accepting a guest was an easy way of getting a can of drink or bar of chocolate from the visitors' canteen.

One day I confronted him in his cell. It started a vicious row. He cursed Michael and cursed God, which made me really angry. 'Tell me, preacher,' he spat, 'where is your Jesus here in this cell, in this filthy hellhole?' I replied through gritted teeth, coming up close to him.

'Jesus is visiting you through Michael . . . '

'Ha! That weakling piece of rubbish, with his church talk and his stupid smile and his books and letters. I'd like to drag him down here and show him what it's really all about.'

I could feel the old anger rising inside me, getting out of control. I grabbed him by the shirt. 'Say one more thing about Michael like that and I'll smash your teeth in.'

'C'mon then preacher, do it,' he grinned, pushing his face out towards me. I did. It wasn't a full force hit, but I slapped him across the mouth, sending him flying onto the table. For weeks, Ziggy had been working on a scale model of a large yacht, based on a picture that Chico, one of the Spanish inmates, had given him. It was in its final stages, beautifully decorated and standing proudly on the table. As Ziggy fell, the model smashed to the ground, splintering into thousands of pieces.

Ziggy leapt back at me in a red-hot rage. I slapped him again and this time pinned him to the floor. He struggled, cursing me, trying to break free. I yelled above him, 'Ziggy, Ziggy, stop. I'm telling you this because you are my friend. Jesus loves you, he wants to save you.' We struggled on and I kept repeating my words until his grip weakened.

He was crying now. 'I want to believe, I really want to believe. But it's so hard in here. I can't bear it.' His large body quivered and he broke down before me. My heart ached. Prison was hard. Every day I watched it break the toughest of men. There were suicides and men going out of their minds in desperation and loneliness, right before our eyes. We both wept.

'Ziggy, let's pray,' I said. 'Right here and now. I don't know what else to do, what else to tell you. Will you pray with me?'

Ziggy nodded weakly, and God's presence soon broke through the misery and squalor of the tiny cell.

In the weeks that followed, some of the toughest and meanest men were brought to their knees before Almighty God. An understanding of 'sin' came easily. These men had no difficulty coming to terms with their wrongdoing. The weight of their conviction was some-times overwhelming. Many cried like babies as they thanked Jesus for his forgiveness; for the grace of God that was setting them free in the very depths of their prison cells.

Michael Wright was busier than ever. My mission was to befriend the men and get them to send a visiting order so that Michael could come and meet them. At one time he was visiting more than ten inmates, whilst still feeding me with his wisdom and understanding of Scripture. His church was praying, too. Valerie visited one day and told me they were praying that more Christians would come into the prison so that our small group would swell in number and be a strong support for one another. I was horrified. 'No!' I implored. 'Don't pray anyone into this place. Just pray that the wretched souls already within the bars will come to know Christ.'

One such case was Mohammed, a Muslim. He was a big man with big problems, serving a life sentence for murdering a Greek taxi driver. His wife, Tammam, and brother, Ahmed, were also serving time. Tammam, who was pregnant, was in Nicosia's women's block. I watched Mohammed, week after week, join the Imam for prayers. Some of the Muslims literally had dents in their foreheads from their ritualistic bowing. One day, I beckoned to him as he walked back to his cell with his ragged prayer mat under his arm. 'Come talk to me, Mohammed,' I smiled. Mohammed was a loner. He was hated by the Greeks. He had murdered one of their own and received a hard time from both prisoners and *varianos* because of it. At the same time, he was ostracised by the Muslims because he had brought shame to his family by involving his wife and brother. He had to guard himself well in the prison and was suspicious of everyone. Mohammed looked at me through narrow, untrusting eyes whenever I approached him, but as the weeks went by, I continued to offer him the hand of friendship.

He needed someone. I gave him cigarettes and painting materials and slowly he began to open up.

This particular day Mohammed looked as though the weight of the world was bearing down on him. His yellow-stained fingers shook as he lit a cigarette. 'Allah has turned his back on me, Tony,' he said, tears welling in his eyes. 'I don't know what to do any more.'

'Tell me about it,' I said, silently asking Jesus for guidance. He lowered his voice to a whisper.

'I've heard awful things about the women's prison and I'm terrified for Tammam.'

'What do you mean?'

'I hear the officers rape and abuse the women.' Mohammed swallowed hard, slowly shaking his head and dragging heavily on the cigarette. 'Our baby is due to be born soon. I will probably never see it.'

'You will get out of here one day. A life sentence doesn't mean life.'

'My life won't be worth living when I get out of here. Tammam's family are trying to get her to divorce me. I don't know what to say to her.'

'Will you be able to see her?'

'There is a visit arranged next week, if the *chowishi* allows it to go ahead. We will have half an hour in a room together. I don't know if I will be able to look her in the face.'

'I will pray for you.'

'Pray to your God, Tony, for what good it will do.' He pushed his prayer mat aside, giving it a light kick. 'Even my family has turned against me. I know what I did was wrong, but I was desperate. I was offered big money to kill that Greek. It would have fed my family for a year. Every day in Jordan, I watched my mother and father, brothers, sisters and cousins struggle to put food on the table. They need me to provide. I don't know what will happen to them.' Mohammed hid his face in his hands and we sat together in silence.

A few days later I was watching Michael Wright leave when I saw a Muslim woman in the visitors' reception area. She was heavily pregnant and accompanied by a female *variano* who was helping herself to coffee at the canteen. It had to be Tammam. It was a sweltering hot day and the other *varianos* were relaxed and lethargic. Quickly, I approached her. She spoke very little English, but I managed to communicate. 'I'm a friend of your husband,' I said, smiling and pointing at myself. 'Mohammed, good friend, good man.' She smiled, looking nervously toward her guard. I handed her a scrap of paper with Michael's details scribbled on it. 'Ask this man to visit you. He will help you,' I said. I could not be certain that she understood, but there was nothing more I could do. The *variano* had spotted us and began shouting for me to move away. Five days later, Michael told me in a letter that he had received a visiting order from Tammam. As I expected, he set to work, visiting her and organising some of the women from his church to support her.

One day Mohammed burst into my cell. He was flustered and nervous, sweating profusely. 'I have had a note from Tammam,' he said. It was not unheard of that men and women prisoners could pass illicit notes to one another. Occasionally, we would catch sight of the women walking past the gates when we were in the courtyard at exercise times. Some of the *varianos* turned a blind eye, so small exchanges could take place.

'She says she has put her trust in your Jesus,' Mohammed said frantically. 'Have you any idea what this means? If my brother Ahmed finds out, the whole family and the rest of our village will know. She will be killed as soon as she is released from here.'

It was hard to talk to Mohammed that day. He was angry and distraught, but there was also something else going on, and I knew it. He, too, had been persuaded to see Michael. Sure enough, only a few days later, Mohammed sought me out again. It was the first time I had seen him with a smile on his face. He looked younger and his eyes were wide and bright. His worries were not over, but like me, he had found his Saviour. Despite his circumstances, he had a reason to live and a new hope. He knew he could trust in God for his wife's safety. We became powerful prayer partners.

The prison's 'official religion' was that of the Greek Orthodox. Other religions were tolerated and there was a large Muslim population. The authorities deemed it heresy, however, to preach the Bible's teaching, that all must be 'born again' through Jesus Christ. I didn't care. I was desperate to share the good news of what I had found with anyone, including the *varianos*.

Still, we had to be careful about our gatherings. By now there was quite a group of new Christians wanting to meet together to pray and share communion. Cramming into my tiny cell, we felt like the first disciples of Jesus Christ, who met in secret following his death and resurrection. We studied the early church, adopting their ways and following the teachings of the New Testament as closely as we could. It became important to us to break bread together and share wine whenever we gathered in Jesus' name. This was not always easy, but it seemed that God was truly blessing our desperate endeavours. We never went short. Everyone scavenged for bread and saved the grapes that were occasionally handed out at dinner time. They weren't fit for eating anyway, but crushed through a clean pair of socks and left to ferment, they turned into precious wine, probably very much like Jesus himself served.

I looked around my cell. Men were squashed together on the bed, others squatted on the floor. There was Ziggy and Mohammed, sharing a joke together. Martin, a weak-bodied British journalist, looked punier than ever as he fought for space next to Ziggy. He was serving time for visa fraud and couldn't handle prison at all. From his first day inside, he stuck close to me for protection and quickly fell into the kingdom of God. Next there was Hassan, a drug dealer from Lebanon. Andreas, a big Greek body-builder serving time for manslaughter, and a couple of others.

'Where's Shane?' I asked. 'And Simone?' Just then Simone came charging into the cell, breathless and distressed. 'Alcaponey's had Shane,' he said, fighting to tell us what had happened.

I pushed past him and belted down the block towards Shane's cell. The *varianos* were carrying him out on a stretcher. Other men gathered around and I pushed through them trying to reach my friend. He was barely conscious and quivering in shock. His trousers were torn and hanging in tatters around his ankles and his shirt was a mass of red that dripped onto the floor in puddles. Deep purple bruises covered his arms and legs and his upper torso oozed blood through vicious razor cuts. His face, 'Oh, dear Lord, his face,' I gasped. It was hardly recognisable.

A curtain of red-hot anger fell over me.

I had been free of it for months, but now, suddenly I was the old Tony again: fierce, furious and spitting. As I watched the *varianos* take Shane away, I vowed to break Alcaponey into a million pieces. That all too familiar metallic tang came back into my mouth. I wanted his blood.

Chapter 12

I beat my fist into the wall, sending crumbling plaster splintering in all directions. The other men parted like waves when I spun around to head back towards my cell. Too angry to pray, I marched around the block for hour after hour until finally, in the privacy of my cell, I fell to the floor, grieving for my brutalised friend and brother. For days afterwards I wrestled with God. I read my Bible, but I was blinded by anger. I prayed that I would be given the opportunity to take revenge for Shane. I wanted to kill Alcaponey, and told God so, in no uncertain terms. I could never forgive him . . . never. I wouldn't rest until I had beaten the life out of him. As for Shane, I feared he would never recover.

When I gave my life to Christ, on the 3 May 1990, I had been set free. Though the prison bars still held me, I had a new freedom that was better than any physical release. My encounter with Alcaponey, however, was to teach me several hugely important lessons. I was soon to be brought to my knees again, this time in awe and wonder at the all-powerful, all-present God, who knows me better than I know myself.

Alcaponey knew I was after him. We were both waiting for the moment when we would come face to face. It came nearly two weeks later, in a darkened and deserted enclave of the wing.

Nicosia Central Prison was built primarily by the

Turks who, at the time, had little regard for health, safety or general living standards. It had many dead end corridors and blocked up ancient passageways that remained largely deserted by the men. In the new darkness of my soul I had taken to seeking them out. Lurking in the silent squalor I wrestled with my rage, plotting my revenge and fine-tuning the details of the damage I would inflict on Alcaponey. There was no room for God here. I was alone, once more, with my demons of destruction.

Suddenly, a blood-curdling obscenity bounced off the walls and Alcaponey's heaving form came out of the darkness. How had he caught me so unaware? Still, I locked my eyes to his and grinned in sick pleasure as he pinned me against the wall. Now was my chance to smash him. Now I could take revenge for Shane's beating. Now I could settle a million scores, breaking this brute into pieces until his flesh became one with the concrete. The taste rose in my mouth and I savoured its sting. I called on the Ch'i and assessed his body, his every potential move through the way of Kung Fu. It felt good. He held a blade tight against my throat but it meant nothing. I didn't care if I lived or died. I would take him first. It was simply a case of how I could do the most damage.

The drive to taste his blood was becoming overwhelming. I knew to strike at his face: his mouth, his nose, his eyes, his ears. Yes, his right ear was open and ready for the taking . . .

> Then the men stepped forward, seized Jesus and arrested him. With that, one of Jesus' companions reached for his sword, drew it out and struck the servant of the high priest, cutting off his ear.

"Put your sword back in its place," Jesus said to him, "for all who draw the sword will die by the sword. Do you think I cannot call on my Father, and he will at once put at my disposal more than twelve legions of angels? . . . " (Matthew 26:50–53)

Only that morning I had read in my Bible about Jesus' arrest in the garden of Gethsemane. Now, in the heat of the attack, the story flooded into my mind. That wasn't all. Instinctively, I was drawing my power from the way of Kung Fu, but Jesus' words were also ringing in my head. 'I am the way and the truth and the life . . . I am the way . . . I am the way . . . I am *the way*.'

The battle raged within as Alcaponey's hammy face stuck to mine. I tasted the salt of his sweat.

'I am *the* way . . . I am the way.'

'Take him now! His ear, bite it! Rip it off!'

'All who draw the sword . . . '

'For Shane . . . don't let yourself be that way . . . do it for Shane . . . '

' . . . the truth, the life . . . '

Suddenly, words formed in my mouth. I heard myself speak. My terror was gone. My lust for Alcaponey's blood evaporated as I spoke. I was suddenly calm, yet as shocked as the brute by the power of my utterance:

'In the name of the Lord Jesus Christ, I command you to leave me alone.'

Moments later I allowed myself to slowly slide down the wall, first squatting on my haunches, then sitting, with my elbows on my knees and my head in my hands. Alcaponey was gone. I half expected him to return, but minutes went by and there was no sign of him. I was bewildered and dazed. Slowly, realisation came to me. God had moved in a miraculous way. He had protected me and I hadn't even asked him to. I hadn't got close to a prayer, but God knew the words before I even considered speaking them. I tried to piece it all together. I had given my life to God and now I was his child. He didn't need me to ask for his help, he stepped in and saved me, despite myself.

I was dumbstruck, just like the first apostles when they saw for themselves the reality of God's Son. In the book of Acts, chapter 1, Jesus' followers were waiting in Jerusalem, as he had asked them to, in anticipation of receiving the power of the Holy Spirit. We are told, ' . . . he was taken up before their very eyes, and a cloud hid him from their sight. They were looking intently up into the sky as he was going, when suddenly two men dressed in white stood beside them . . . '

Such was the presence of God, enfolding me in that filthy, squalid corridor, that I might easily have seen angels.

Walking slowly back towards the main block, I remained shrouded in the mighty power of God. It was almost tangible. I marvelled at what had happened. I knew that I had spoken to Alcaponey in English, yet this barbarian was barely able to speak Greek, his own language, never mind anything else. As I reached my cell I gazed again at the shape of the cross, formed by the window bars. 'I am the way and the truth and the life . . . ' I feasted on the words and knew it had not been the Ch'i or martial arts that had saved me. It had been Jesus and my God-given faith that shielded me from clear and present danger. It was my first, scariest, most powerful lesson in faith. I knew it was time to fully turn my back on the way of Kung Fu and put my trust firmly in the hands of God.

Over the years I have remembered that incident many times as a pivotal point in my life. It is often said that 'prayer changes things', but to that, I will always say, 'no, prayer doesn't change things, God does.' In the Gospel of Mark, chapter 11, Jesus discloses the secret to true prayer: 'Have faith in God,' he says – not faith in faith, or faith in prayer, but 'faith in God'. Wrestling with Alcaponey, I could have easily taken things into my own hands. I could have crushed him, using my own skill and training, but God was honouring my decision to follow him. In the heat of the moment, he gave me the strength to set myself aside and to trust only in him.

I knew it was time to tell my Chinese family of my decision to follow Christ. I wrote to my grandfather, knowing full well the severity of my words. In turning my back on martial arts, I was destroying his legacy, denying my heritage and breaking the sacred vows to preserve the ancient way of Kung Fu. I hoped that when I told Lowsi of my new, life-saving faith, he would come to a gracious understanding. However, deep down, I knew that the consequence of this letter would more likely leave me with a bounty on my head for the rest of my earthly life. I had known it before. Anyone raised in the traditional way who denies the way of Kung Fu, defiles its legacy or corrupts its original purpose, is always brought to task. I knew that my family would arrange a council to approach me, expecting me to retract my denial of the art and seek their pardon. They would send an opponent to fight me so that I could prove myself once more as worthy of my title and heritage. If I refused the challenge, I would be hunted down and made to submit, possibly with my life.

Weeks passed by before a letter arrived. It was from my cousin, Si Kwon. Her tone was cold and harsh. She told me our grandfather had died. He was 95. Si Kwon wrote of the shame I had brought to the family by not being with them, paying homage to our ancestors, at this time. The letter went on to demand that I deny my Christian faith and continue the honourable teaching of my heritage. As the only male descendant of Cheung Ling Soo, our family's honour lay solely on my shoulders. It was just as I predicted.

The news of Lowsi's death shook me. I didn't know how I should feel. I had hated him for most of my life, yet he had left his mark on me. He had given me an identity. I knew that, in his death, something of me was also gone forever. Furthermore, by not responding to Si Kwon's demands I realised that I would be severing my links with my Chinese family forever. What did that really mean? Could I live permanently looking over my shoulder? It was likely that the family would hire Triads to come after me. Yet my new life, my faith and God's protection, were so real and more powerful than anything my grandfather had taught me. There would be no going back. I pictured my grandfather's face and tried to remember the better times we had together, and the respect I had for him in later years. I remained emotionally numb.

Word quickly got around the wing that Alcaponey had escaped me and that I had turned my back on the way of Kung Fu. Some of the lunatics tried to take advantage, but God continued to protect me in a miraculous way. Among the more sane men, I seemed to be earning a deep respect. Apparently, the transformation in my character was obvious and, at the same time, intriguing.

Several years ago, Chicago newspapers carried the story of a delivery boy in a Chinese restaurant who went to a bank to get change for $500. The restaurant needed $250 in coins and $250 in $1 bills. The cashier grabbed a stack of $100 bills by mistake and gave the delivery boy $250 in coins and $25,000 in bills.

The delivery boy noticed the error immediately, but detecting a windfall, didn't say anything. He left the bank with the money and hid it at a relative's home. He then returned to the restaurant, thinking he had made a small fortune.

The cashier, when she discovered her mistake, couldn't identify the person to whom she had given the $100 bills. But she remembered how he smelled. She knew from his scent that he worked in a Chinese restaurant. She not only remembered the aroma, but she was able to connect it with the exact restaurant where the boy worked. With the police, she located the restaurant and identified the delivery boy. He was promptly fired and the money was recovered.

I thought about this story as I studied the Bible, discovering what it means to sincerely follow Christ. The apostle Paul wrote, 'For we are to God the aroma of Christ among those who are being saved and those who are perishing' (2 Corinthians 2:15). The aroma Paul is talking about is not one detected with the nose. It is something that is sensed by those who come in contact with us.

Aroma is usually a by-product of activity. I was used to the odour of sweat from my training in Kung Fu. When you eat garlic, you get garlic breath. If you douse yourself with perfume, you smell like the fragrance counter in a department store. In the same way, when you serve Jesus, and do it in a spirit of love and humility, you begin to pick up the aroma of Christ.

Almost every day I found myself in conversation with new prisoners and even some of the *varianos*. Many were coming to me with questions and problems. Most were utterly broken on the wheels of life, facing horrible addictions or heartbreaking family issues and dilemmas. Miraculously, I seemed to be given the wisdom to help them. With some I prayed and read the Bible, revealing the way God speaks directly to us, through Scripture. I continued to urge each man to send a visiting order to Michael Wright, knowing he could help them, as he had helped me.

One day I received a letter from Michael with some very bad news. He had been given notice by the prison that he could no longer visit. By that time he was regularly seeing ten *fylakismenos*, and some of his church members were visiting the women's block. He was our lifeline. I could tell by the tone of the letter that he was desperately upset, but he urged us to be strong. 'Spend time in prayer,' he wrote. 'Seek God's understanding of this situation. If it is his will, pray that I will soon be allowed to return.' I knew Michael was pouring everything of himself into supporting us. Each time he visited, it was a two hour round trip in the blazing Cyprus heat. Often, he had to pull over to rest at the roadside on his way home. Each meeting left him exhausted by the burden of the lives he was reaching. Still, he kept on, empowered through his weakness, by the God he was serving.

I was indebted to Michael for my life. If it had not been for his visits I would not have heard the message of Jesus Christ. Quickly, I gathered the group together. We broke bread, thanking Jesus for his sacrifice, then fell to our knees, begging God to allow Michael to come back into the prison.

I put in a request to see the *chowishi* and, after days of prayer, found myself standing before him to argue the case. 'I hear good things, Tony,' he said. 'The *varianos* tell me you are a changed man.'

'Yes, I'm a Christian now.'

'This is, how you call, "born again"?' He waved his hand dismissively and smirked.

'Yes,' I said. I longed to tell him more, but I knew his game. He was mocking me and I knew I was on dangerous ground. 'Sir,' I ventured, speaking in Greek, 'there are many men who are being helped by the visits of Michael Wright.' He wiped his brow with his handkerchief and gestured that I continue. 'I am sure the *varianos* have told you how much calmer many of the men are. We mean no trouble. There is less violence on the block.'

'This is what I have heard, yes.'

'Then please, sir, let Michael return,' I said, hoping and praying that his heart would soften.

Two weeks later, Michael was allowed back into the *fylaki*. We thanked God for a mighty answer to prayer. Not only was Michael able to visit, but he was given special permission to come into the library where he could lead group studies. Richard Knox also came, bringing his trumpet along to lead us in hymns and songs of praise. I will never forget those meetings.

Still, it came with a cost. I had served nearly two and a half years of my three-year sentence. Everyone expected that I would be released any day on remission. Again I found myself before the *chowishi*.

He wore the same smirk. 'I still hear good things, Tony. And you have your man, this Michael Wright.'

'Yes, sir, thank you.' I wondered why he was talking about this, rather than the subject of my release.

'Sir,' I ventured, 'I'm wondering when I will receive notification of my release. Should I not be up for remission soon?'

The *chowishi* grinned wickedly. 'Well, you have your preacher man and I have been very good to you . . . ' He let his words hang, as though expecting more praise and thanks. I said nothing. 'But, you see, the authorities take what you have been up to very seriously.'

'Sir?'

'All this teaching from your Bible, you have been preaching heresy and for that you have lost your remission. You will serve your full three-year sentence.' I was annoyed, but not altogether surprised. Michael had talked to me about the threat from the Greek Orthodox Church which was very powerful in the *fylaki*. I could not, and would not, remain angry. There were many men to reach and I knew that Michael's visits could be stopped again at any moment.

Each morning, in the silence before dawn, I spoke with God. I prayed for many prisoners by name, making detailed requests. Many prayers were answered immediately, but with each day my heart ached more and more. There was such incredible need among the men. Some days I felt almost physical pain as my eyes were opened to the deep hurt and torture that had turned ordinary men into murderers, rapists and madmen. Here among the filth, the noise, the foul smells and the human degradation were desperate, truly tormented individuals.

The prison ran a carpentry and print shop, where some of the more able and skilled prisoners worked. Most of us had some kind of job. Mine was usually cleaning or serving food. For some reason, Gazantha, the Arab barber, was allowed to set up his business in the carpentry area. 'Ah Tony, my friend, come sit down,' he greeted me, with his wide-mouthed grin. 'You want your usual?'

'Yes, my friend, I'm feeling brave today. You watch that blade doesn't slip though.'

'Ah, you know I give you the best shave in the whole of Nicosia.' We laughed and chatted together as he began clipping my beard. Through the tiny cracked mirror I watched the men working the machines of the carpenters' shop. There was a lot of noise: the machines, men calling to one another, singing. My attention was drawn to Kyriacos, a small Greek man. He was standing very still by the circular saw. I watched him for a while. He wasn't operating the machine, but just staring into the blade. Everything else was going on around him. Gazantha continued to chat, but I grew suddenly very troubled. I couldn't take my eyes off Kyriacos. In horror, I watched as he slowly put his hand into the blade. One by one, his fingers and thumb fell to the floor. He barely flinched, nor made a sound. I spun around in the chair and flew over to him.

Noticing the commotion, the other workers dropped what they were doing. When they saw what had happened many of the Greeks and Arabs began wailing and tearing at their clothing in distress. Kyriacos remained standing, as if in a trance, with his hand still raised. The machine was still running, covering everyone with smatterings of blood. Noise. Chaos. Panic. No one knew what to do. Tears began to run down Kyriacos' face, then he whimpered and began to fall. The *chowishi* of the workshop caught him before he hit the stone and summoned for assistance. In the chaos I rummaged around in the red stained sawdust, trying to retrieve the severed fingers.

It was an utterly sickening experience. The *fylaki* could drive any man to distraction and madness. Kyriacos had heard that his wife was having an affair. He had also recently lost certain privileges, his paints and paper. It had tipped him over the edge. Such horrific, deliberate acts of self-destruction were far too common.

Violence was commonplace, but the bloodshed and terror that once gave me a rush, now sickened me to the core. The *fylaki* was an emotional tinderbox. One man's grievance could easily light the touchpaper and, before you knew it, a huge fight exploded on the wing. These days I took rapid cover in my cell. There was a time when I relished the opportunity to lay into the prisoners who got on my nerves. That's the way everyone used these fights. They were a great release, but they were bloody and violent and I knew I had to stay away.

The summer of 1992 was unbearably hot and it did nothing for the general mood on the wing. The men were irritable and restless and many of us knew there was another big rumble brewing between the Palestinians and the Greeks. When it came, there were many casualties. As usual, the various factions were isolated from one another and I found myself, once again, visiting Palestinian friends in solitary confinement.

'There will be an investigation,' Ian Davidson told me as I served him from the *Lamarina*. The guards on duty that day were OK – they wouldn't bother us.

'Why, what happened?' I asked.

'Some Greek guy got badly hurt. They say he might not come round.'

'So. What's different this time?'

'He was a man of influence. Some kind of politician we think.' I handed him a rather grey-looking over-boiled egg and a plate of stale tomatoes. 'How much longer can we take this, Tony?' he smiled.

'I put in your order for a pie and a pint, so maybe tomorrow, eh?' I teased.

'Did you hear there were a couple of journalists sniffing around?'

'Yeah?'

'Tried to pose as officials, but they didn't get very far.'

'Still, it's good to know the outside world hasn't forgotten about us.'

'Yeah, but this one could have repercussions for the cause. We don't want our names all over the papers again.'

'No one will talk will they?'

'Rumour has it there's already been a grass. We just need to find out who.'

A *variano* was coming towards us. 'Time's up, mate,' I said. 'See you tomorrow.'

I struggled to turn the *Lamarina* around. 'Don't forget that pie and a pint of John Smith's Best,' Ian said with a wink.

A few days later, I found myself in a whispered conversation with Ian's brother-in-arms, Adli. He was one of the ringleaders. A one-time bodyguard to Yasser Arafat, he was a highly respected member of the PLO. He had become something of a friend, but I knew a liaison with him would be dangerous. Adli was scribbling on a tiny scrap of paper as I served his food. Slipping the note through the bars he looked at me intently. 'This man is the one, Tony,' he said, furtively. 'The grass.'

'What?'

'The grass. From our own land,' he spat.

'What, a Palestinian?'

'Yeah,' he lowered his voice, 'but not one of us.' He tapped the side of his head, gesturing that the traitor was not intelligent enough to be part of the imprisoned PLO elite. 'Everyone hates a grass, Tony. We need to deal with him.'

'Adli, you know I don't . . . '

'Come on Tony,' he interrupted. 'We're mates. None of us can do it from in here can we? He needs to be taught a serious lesson.'

To my relief, the *varianos* shouted at me to get a move on. I pushed the scrap of paper into my pocket and, without looking at Adli, manoeuvred the *Lamarina* back down towards the light. I never looked at the name on the paper. It went straight in the fire.

There was no way I was getting involved in this one. But I should have known there would be others only too willing.

Several days later, I was walking in the courtyard. The air was getting cooler and it was welcome relief after the months of torturous heat. Two Palestinians, Hussain and Yousef, passed by. I thought nothing of it. They greeted me. I smiled and, lost in my thoughts, walked on around the perimeter of the yard. As I circled back towards them I stopped. What was he doing? The youngest of the men, Hussain, had pulled his companion backwards over a bench by the hair. He stood over him, jamming his hand into his face. In horror I realised he had a blade. For a moment I couldn't move. The young man chopped and sliced madly as Yousef kicked and yelled, blood spurting from his face.

'Stop! Stamada! Hallus, hallus!' I cried. I ran, but by the time I got close, Hussain had fled back into the block. Yousef's body slumped backwards over the bench, unconscious and quivering. His face was a mass of red. I pulled him onto the floor and realised he had stopped breathing. Close protection training kicked in. With his features in shreds, I struggled even to find his mouth. I breathed deeply into him. 'Please God, bring him back.' I heard running footsteps and continued to try to resuscitate him. His body jerked and blood-filled vomit exploded over me. 'Wait.' I told the *varianos* who came running to my aid. I flipped Yousef onto his side and put him in a recovery position. Medics arrived a few moments later. It was then I started to shake. I had saved the man's life, but who knows what kind of recovery he could make from that.

In the midst of such violence I was beginning to see very clearly the way God was protecting the group of new Christians. We lived our lives under constant threat of the blade; of madmen who would throw hot oil or boiling sugared water in your face as easy as look at you. Trusting in God was easy in the *fylaki*. There was no doubting his heavenly protection and provision.

The time for my release was drawing near. I had served my full three-year sentence. I knew God was preparing the way for me. He had a plan. Somehow, deep in my spirit, I knew that I had to cut myself free from any links with my past. It seemed that God was telling me to trust him completely, to throw away all my old contacts and start afresh, relying totally on him.

He proved himself quickly, helping me to overcome a number of instant hurdles. My passport had expired and I needed money to get out of the country. There were many men still rotting in the *fylaki* long after their sentences had ended, simply because they had no funds to leave.

Michael Wright and Richard Knox visited me for the last time in Nicosia Central Prison. 'The next time we're together, it will be on the outside,' smiled Michael.

'We've been in touch with the British embassy and a passport is being arranged for you,' Richard told me. 'I'm also leaving a plane ticket, in your name, with the administration office here. You'll pick them both up on Wednesday.'

I didn't know how to thank him. We sat in silence for a little while, Michael with that beautiful smile beaming all over his face. 'God will take care of you, Tony,' he said. I nodded, but I had no idea what was ahead.

'I've been in touch with my friend, Cor Bruins,' Richard told me. 'We were missionaries together in Lebanon.' I'd heard Richard talk of the Dutchman and his family before. 'Cor's daughter, Carolyn, has offered to put you up when you get back to England.' Richard pulled a small envelope from his jacket pocket. It held a photograph of a family. They were all smiling. 'This is Carolyn and her husband, John,' Richard pointed out, 'and their two children, 2-year-old Anna and baby Joshua.' I was suddenly and very painfully aware of the innocence and beauty of the family. Richard continued chattering about them. 'They live in New Malden, Surrey, where they're part of a Baptist church . . . '

'Do they know who I am, what I've done?' I interrupted. I felt anxious and disturbed. Richard smiled in assurance.

'Remember, Tony, "There is no condemnation for those who are in Christ Jesus,"' he said, quoting Scripture. 'They are a lovely Christian family. They are not going to judge you. They know that you are being released from here and they've promised to pick you up from the airport and take you to their home.' He dug into the envelope again and pulled out a short letter. It was from Carolyn and John saying how much they were looking forward to meeting me. They told me their house was small, but that I would be comfortable and very much welcomed. I was overwhelmed by the generosity of these strangers.

Chapter 13

It was 11 November 1992. Release day. Long before dawn I opened my daily devotional. In the flickering candlelight I stared in amazement at the page. The title of the reading for the day was 'Free Indeed.' I feasted on the words of John 8:36. It was my verse. I knew that God had seen me every step of the way. Now, I had to trust him for my future.

I spent the morning going around the block, talking to as many men as possible, urging them to give their lives to Jesus. Saying goodbye to my friends was very difficult. We had shared so much together. Ziggy, Simone, Ian, Martin, Andreas, Hassan . . . There were tears in Mohammed's eyes. 'Keep trusting, my friend,' I said. 'We are free men.' I grasped his hand and left it over his heart, in a final embrace.

Taking one last look at the block, I turned and began a slow walk to the outside world.

In the *chowishi*'s office I rifled through the small bag of my belongings. I was thankful to put on a decent pair of shoes, though they felt tight and stiff after wearing flip-flops for three years. There was a pair of jeans and a black polo-neck sweater. For a few moments I stood, contemplating and fingering the three little red books. They were full of names, numbers and addresses: all my old work and Kung Fu contacts. Reminding myself of God's promise, I dropped them in the waste bin. Now I filled the bag with my Emmaus course books, my Bible and a few other books Michael had brought into the prison for me. I left many others behind for my friends. There was one book I will always hang on to, *Through Gates of Splendour*. I smiled to myself, remembering that night in the holding cell when I had met the Nigerian man. I often thought about him. Who was he really? Could he have been someone sent by God, an angel even? I was certain that he had written his name and his address in Lagos on the inside cover of the book. Yes, I had seen it that night, with my own eyes. Yet, since then, I had looked for his scribbled writing numerous times. No pages had been torn out, but there was no sign of his markings. It remains a mystery.

The *chowishi* handed me an envelope containing a passport and ticket. For a moment I was transported back to my days with the close protection unit. Locked in an account in Switzerland there was, and probably still is, a stack of false passports, giving me numerous nationalities and identities. Getting false documents was easy if you knew the right people. Now I held a passport issued by the British consulate, but it was very badly put together. There was a scribbled note with it from Richard. 'We are very grateful to a lady at the embassy for this item. You will need to get it updated when you are in England, but it will get you out of the country for now.' I cringed, looking at the dreadful photograph I'd had taken in prison. I stuffed it into my back pocket, along with the ticket to London's Heathrow airport. 'Let's go,' I said to the *varianos*.

Five policemen escorted me to Larnaca airport. I would be blacklisted in Cyprus for five years and they had to be certain I was leaving the country. From the back of the car I drank in the scenes. Blue sky, trees, mountains, women, children, the smell of the sea. I had kept these images in my head for three long years. Now I was seeing them again for real. My senses were

heightened to everything of the outside world, everything I had missed.

I was detained in a police office at the airport until the
flight was ready to depart. Suddenly, I heard a familiar
voice. It was Michael Wright. He and his father-in-law had
driven out to the airport to bid me farewell. They brought
me a heavy overcoat. 'It was Elizabeth's idea,' Michael
smiled. 'She reminded me England will be very cold.' He
opened his Bible, taking me through some key passages,
encouraging me and building me up. It was as though I
was his child and he was seeing me off into the world. Our
parting was emotional. He had given me so much. Michael
had stepped out of his church to go in search of the lost
and needy. Leaving the security of his own people, he had
moved to a foreign country, trusting in God's calling. Not
only had he faced cultural barriers, but he had then dared
to step right into the firing line. Nicosia Central Prison was
home to the meanest of the mean, the last place on earth
for a nice man like him. And yet he had been faithful. He
had loved the lost, as Jesus did, and brought hope and life
to the desperate and most forsaken. As far as I could
understand, he had done exactly what Jesus calls us all to
do. He had laid his own needs aside and set out to reach
people like me with the good news of Jesus Christ. Michael
had set a standard by which I would later measure many
of the people I met in churches in the UK. Sadly, it set me
up for a rude awakening.

I had been on many aeroplanes in my life, but now I
gazed in wonder and awe at the lights below as the
plane rose into the clouds. It was beautiful. Life was
beautiful. I closed my eyes and thought back over the
last three years. I was full, and thankful.

As the plane began to descend, my limbs trembled
with a mixture of fear and excitement. To calm myself I
recited the words of Psalm 23 in my head:

The Lord is my shepherd, I shall lack nothing. He makes
me lie down in green pastures, he leads me beside quiet
waters, he restores my soul. He guides me in paths of
righteousness for his name's sake. Even though I walk
through the valley of the shadow of death, I will fear no
evil, for you are with me; your rod and your staff, they
comfort me. You prepare a table before me . . . Surely
goodness and love will follow me all the days of my life,
and I will dwell in the house of the Lord for ever.

As I walked through the arrivals gate I instantly
recognised John and Carolyn Nunn and their children. I
was painfully aware of what a shady character I must
have appeared. I could barely look them in the face, but
they embraced me, as though I were some long lost
family member. It was hard to know what to say. My
senses were being bombarded with life. After three years
in a dungeon, everything seemed big and loud, frightening even. The car journey left me feeling nauseous, but I
was so grateful to these people, this ordinary family,
who laughed and chatted and tried to make me feel
welcome. Inside their house, my unease remained. I was
almost dizzy. It was warm and there was the smell of
cooking. There were family photographs everywhere,
comfy chairs and children's toys littering the floor. It was
so normal, yet so strange and difficult to take in.

John showed me around the house, leaving me alone
in the small guest room they had prepared. Carolyn
shouted from the kitchen that dinner would be on the
table in fifteen minutes. I suddenly realised I was ravenously hungry. I sat on the edge of the bed, fingering the
soft, clean linen, looking at the pictures on the walls, the
fresh towels and toiletries that had been put out for me.
It was all so perfect, so undeserved. 'These people have
no idea,' I thought, catching sight of myself in the mirror.

I took a luxurious hot shower. Three years of ingrained dirt slipped down the drain. Washing in the *fylaki* was a dangerous affair. There were always lurid eyes watching and to strip naked could be a very bad move. You could never rely on hot water either. Sometimes it would be off for days at a time, then dirty brown liquid would come clattering out of the ancient pipes and we would all fight for space at the taps.

Downstairs there was music on the stereo and Anna was running around, escaping her dad who was trying to put her in a high chair. 'Come and sit down,' he laughed, noticing me at the door. 'Make yourself at home.' He picked up the toddler and swung her by her ankles, upside down until she squealed with delight. Then spinning her around he secured her, next to me, in the chair. She looked at me and laughed, then pretended to be shy, hiding her face and peeking out from between her fingers.

Carolyn came in with a steaming saucepan and plonked it down on the table. 'I'm not going to apologise for bringing the saucepan to the table, Tony.' I looked at her puzzled. 'You're not a guest, you're family, and I'm afraid, this is how we serve our food.' With that she spooned great quantities of wonderful-smelling casserole onto the plates. John thanked God for the food and we began to eat. It felt so good.

The Nunns were very welcoming, but they could never have understood how strange and difficult I found this 'normal' family set-up. I had never experienced such a family life. Sometimes I struggled to handle the fact that they were so trusting of me. John would go to work and Carolyn would be in another room with baby Joshua, leaving me and their little girl alone in the lounge. I wondered if they could ever imagine the violence that had been so much a part of me.

Anna loved teasing. I'd had no experience of children, but something about her helped ease my nerves. One day Carolyn, frustrated at how long Anna was taking to eat her breakfast, put an egg-timer on the table. 'You must finish by the time the sand runs out Anna, otherwise, there will be trouble.' She left the room and Anna stared into her porridge bowl.

'Don't want,' she said, pushing the dish away and sticking out her bottom lip. I didn't know what to do. I went over and sat beside her.

'Come on Anna, eat it up. It's delicious,' I said, unsure of how to react. She eyed me suspiciously. I took the egg-timer and twisted it, adding a few more minutes. That made Anna smile. 'Sssshh,' I said, winking at her.

'Sssshh,' she said back, putting her finger over her lips. Then she giggled and started quickly eating her porridge. We were friends.

That Sunday, 15 November 1992, I went with the family to New Malden Baptist Church. It was something I had been looking forward to for months. I loved hearing Michael and the other visitors talk about their churches and I knew it would be a real treat to meet so many other Christians. Around three hundred people gathered. Throughout the service I was quite over-whelmed. The welcome and the music was wonderful and when the minister began teaching I tried to hang on to his every word. At one point he invited people to go up and share their testimony. I sat in my seat, shaking for a while, but I knew God was telling me to move. Very anxiously, I stood up and was invited forward. Stuttering and stammering I spilled out some of my story. It was the first time I had spoken like this in public. I had talked to many men in prison, but it had seemed so natural then, so necessary. Now, as I looked out at smiling, encouraging faces, I felt nervous to the point of being ill.

By the end of the morning I had made many new friends and signed myself up for baptism classes. For months I had dreamed of being properly baptised. In prison Michael Wright often talked about the baptisms his church performed at the beach in Cyprus. Ian Reverezer, a young Korean boy, wrote to me describing how he had been baptised in the sea. I was quite jealous. I read in my Bible about John the Baptist baptising Jesus and I knew it was something I needed to do. Whenever possible, I baptised myself as I showered, symbolically dying to my old life, and emerging from the water a new, clean man.

Back at the house I laid the table for Sunday lunch. Two guests had been invited and they both arrived together. They each embraced John and Carolyn as good friends. Phil was around my age, with a broad smile and a firm handshake. We were soon to build a camaraderie based on our shared passion for motorbikes. Sara held out her hand. 'I'm so pleased to meet you,' she said, looking straight into my eyes. 'We've heard so much about you.' I shifted nervously. She smiled and it seemed to light up her whole face. Throughout the meal I was captivated by Sara's radiance. I loved the way she talked with the others about what God was doing in her life. They all appeared to be so in love with Jesus and I knew this was the environment I needed.

That first evening, I couldn't get Sara out of my mind. She was lovely. I smiled every time I thought of her. 'What are you doing?' I asked God. 'I'm not ready for any of this.' I didn't know where it would lead, but I knew Sara was precious. She had made me feel so special that afternoon and I wanted to give her a gift. I took out my calligraphy pens and began to paint.

A few days later I set out for Sara's house. She lived quite a distance away, in Putney. Prison had institutionalised me. I'd travelled the world and managed many itineraries for clients in my close protection security days. Now I was nervous just leaving the house. The thought of getting on a bus or train was more than I could face. The previous day I'd secured a job with a local painter and decorator, just down the road from the Nunns. He'd paid me a day's wages in cash. I spent it all on the taxi fare to Putney.

When I arrived in Sara's street my heart was racing. What was I doing? I held the painting, wrapped in brown paper, and a bunch of flowers. My hands trembled as I reached for the doorbell. She shared the house with four other girls, all student teachers. 'Please Sara, please answer the door,' I whispered to myself as I shuffled uncomfortably on the doorstep. She didn't. There in front of me was a short blonde girl who smirked mischievously when I asked for Sara.

Sara appeared and a couple of other curious faces popped out from the living room. Sara blushed. 'Tony, what a surprise.' I didn't know what to say.

'I just wanted to give you these,' I stammered. I pushed the gifts into her hands and turned to leave.

'Hang on,' she said, somewhat taken aback. 'You can't just go. At least come in for a cup of tea.' I did, though the trembling didn't stop. It didn't stop until long after I had left Sara's house and got back to New Malden. That night I phoned her and we arranged to go out to dinner.

Over the next few weeks we had several dates. I was always racked with nerves, but we talked mostly about our shared faith and that helped put me at ease. Among many of my new friends, I felt ashamed, stupid even, that I had had to go to prison, to the very depths of life, to find God. Here was Sara, a beautiful, good-natured, innocent girl, who had loved Jesus all her life. I was envious of that. She told me she wished she could experience God in the same 'real' way I had. I couldn't understand. I wouldn't wish what I had been through on anyone. Sara had not 'seen' God in the way I had. But I was completely in awe of her apparent 'blind faith' and her beautiful testimony.

Sara had given her life to Jesus when she was still a young child. She smiled as she told me her story. 'I used to love going out with my dad when he was preaching,' she said. 'He wasn't an ordained minister, but in our church all the men are involved in preaching. One night, I'd be around 10 years old, I went with him and I remember him preaching about the "end times". He talked about how the world could end at any time. Jesus will come back, and those who don't believe in him will be left behind.' Sara paused and shivered. 'The thought that I could be one of those left behind really frightened me,' she continued. 'I knew a lot about Jesus and the Bible stories. I knew that I had to believe in Jesus to be saved. I did believe in him, I always had. But I wasn't sure I'd actually made the right kind of commitment. Listening to my dad that night I knew I had to pray the prayer he told everyone about.' I looked at her expectantly and tears seemed to prick in her eyes.

'Yes, I prayed the prayer, Tony,' she said. 'But nothing happened. I'd heard so many times before about how you must pray the prayer and your life will be changed, or you'll have this great feeling of being saved. But for me there was nothing.'

'Nothing?' I queried, remembering that night in my cell when I had first prayed to Jesus.

'No, there was no warm glow, no voice from heaven, no strange feeling. Nothing. I thought I must have done it wrong. Maybe I'd got the words in the wrong order, or maybe I couldn't make my heart mean the prayer sincerely enough,' Sara smiled weakly.

'I was frightened for about a year,' she continued. 'Every night I lay in bed, listening for sounds. Anything would do, just the squeak of a stair, or muffled conversation; anything that would reassure me Mum and Dad were in the house. Sometimes I feigned coughing fits. Mum would come rushing up the stairs and I knew everything was alright, they had not left me. In the silence I feared that Jesus had come and that I had been left behind.' I stared at Sara in amazement. She smiled. 'Eventually I plucked up the courage to talk to Mum and Dad about it. After that, everything was alright.'

'How?' I asked. 'What did they say?'

'Mum explained that all my life they had protected me, that they had not allowed me to become involved with anything that could badly influence my life. I couldn't make any big life change . . . '

'But being saved isn't about living a good life, is it?' I said. I was worried now. There must be more.

'Dad reminded me about the Philippian jailer in the book of Acts,' Sara continued. 'When he saw Paul and Silas being freed from prison by the earthquake he asked them, "What must I do to be saved?" Dad reminded me of their answer: "Believe in the Lord Jesus, and you will be saved." I questioned Dad again, "Is that really all? Are you sure that's all I have to do?" He showed me other verses in the Bible that backed it up. He told me that some people experience very dramatic things when they first come to God, but that it's not like that with everyone. He assured me that it was my ongoing belief and trust in Jesus that really mattered. Somehow, it was what I needed to hear,' Sara finished.

I thought back to my friends in prison. So many of them had come before God with their lives in ruins. I had shared the gospel with them in the only way I had known how. Many times I'd probably got the words very wrong. But I never knew a 'formula', or a particular prayer. None of us had. It saddened me to think of Sara lying awake, fearing that her prayer had been 'wrong'. I knew that words didn't matter, that no heartfelt prayer would go unanswered by God. I remembered Michael Wright's teaching. 'Salvation is given, not earned. Jesus has already done the saving. All we have to do is believe in him and accept his free gift. The way we come to him makes no difference.'

Listening to Sara, I realised how different our lives had been. She had been raised in a loving family with a faith that could almost be taken for granted. I envied her sheltered, innocent life. How could she ever come to terms with who I was, the things I'd done? I was so ashamed. Perhaps, for her sake, it would be better if she had nothing to do with me. Yet there was something about the way Sara listened to me, the way she asked questions and encouraged me. She somehow made me feel valued and precious. I couldn't let her friendship go.

All my adult life I had enjoyed confidence to the point of arrogance. I could walk into a room knowing that, with a snap of a finger, I could be in full command. Since leaving Cyprus that had changed. I had become desperately nervous and stammered and trembled in front of people. Sara must have noticed my awkwardness. I was terrified to touch her in any way. Then, one night she took me by the hand. My first instinct was to pull away, but before I knew it, she reached up and kissed me. I was stunned. At last, the trembling stopped and gave way to overwhelming joy.

After a few months, I moved out of John and Carolyn's house to the home of Alan and Irene Kirkham, a lovely, older couple from the church. From there I took a room in a flat above 'Oak Room', a small gospel hall in Clapham Junction. I'd been there a few days when I realised there was only one other man in the church. The rest of the congregation was made up of middle-aged and elderly black women. Joe McDonald's face was full of relief when he saw me. Since the traditional Brethren church is very strict over the roles of men and women, all the preaching duties had fallen on him. The women were the strength behind the ministry, but when it came to sharing the word and breaking the bread, they had to remain quiet. For years, Joe had faithfully led the church, preaching both morning and evening until he was quite worn out. In only a matter of days I inherited the main share of the work. To my dismay, Joe soon disappeared off the scene all together and I was left with the responsibility. I was truly in at the deep end. By now I had publicly shared my testimony numerous times, but preaching, teaching and leading services was a different matter. The women were strict, and quick to correct me, but they were gracious and I knew that God had placed me there for a reason.

The Brethren are renowned for their Bible knowledge and I spent hour upon hour studying the Scriptures and writing sermons. In the early days, I read my work word for word, until I grew more confident in my preaching techniques. Thankfully, Mike Livingstone, a tall, athletic New Zealander, soon joined me. He had arrived in London soon after me and we quickly became good friends. To my relief, he was welcomed by the women and took his share of the preaching. We often sat up into the early hours sharing stories. Like Sara, Mike had been raised in a Christian home and he, too, was fascinated by my dramatic encounter with Christ. 'Y'know, I used to feel like some-second rate Christian,' he told me one night.

'But you've always known God, how can you say that?' I queried.

'Sure, but I used to worry that I was living my parents' faith, not my own.'

'What do you mean?'

'I've always had to work hard to apply my faith, to claim it as my own,' he said. 'You've really encountered God. I've heard you say you don't need to see any more of God in your life to believe in him.'

'That's right', I replied. 'When I was in prison I knew he was protecting me every moment of the day. It had to be that way for me to survive.'

'But I've never had that. I've never had to truly rely on him, because my life has always been good,' Mike said.

By now I was very familiar with this kind of testimony. It was the same as Sara's. Neither Mike nor Sara could grasp how much I was in awe of them. I could not imagine what it was like to live in such 'blind faith'. Yet they had struggled on, year after year, praising God, trusting him, serving him.

'So what now?' I asked Mike. 'You couldn't do all this in your own strength.' We both felt the weight of preaching and leading in the church and I knew it was God's power that was sustaining us.

'This is what I'm saying, Tony,' Mike smiled. 'My story is very different to yours, but I know my faith is real, it's just that I can't pinpoint any momentous time when I was "converted", the way you can.' This was hard for me to understand, but I knew that Mike was genuine.

'Explain it to me,' I said.

'I was raised in a family who love Jesus, so I grew up knowing what it means to be a Christian, y'know, more than just a church-goer. By the age of 10 I was sure I'd been a Christian for some time. I knew that I'd accepted

Jesus as my saviour; the difficulty was I couldn't remember when I had made this gradual realisation and choice. I just knew that, somehow, I'd made it. I couldn't remember a day when I first trusted in Jesus, basically because I couldn't really remember a day when I did not trust him.' Mike smiled.

'That just seems so strange to me,' I said. 'I suppose because my life was so wrong before, so God had to make a big impact with me.'

'Yeah, maybe,' said Mike. 'Some people have likened conversion to travelling on a train between two countries,' Mike continued. 'If you're awake you may know exactly when you crossed the border, but if you're asleep you will not remember when you passed into the country of your destination. You still made it there though. In my case I just can't remember "becoming" a Christian.'

'Doesn't that leave you open to doubts though?' I asked.

'I suppose that's one of the difficulties I've hit over the years. When I was 13, I was sure that God had asked me to get baptised as an outward sign of my trust in him. So I was baptised. But then, over my teenage years I had a few niggling doubts about the validity of it all. Not being able to remember a definite date of conversion was the main issue, especially when I kept meeting people whose experience of God was more like your own.'

I smiled sadly. 'So?'

'Well, I guess these worries were generally sorted through prayer. There's no harm in asking for forgiveness again, is there?' Mike laughed. 'I suppose the other thing with not having one of these "big experiences" of God is that I really wanted to be able to explain his existence scientifically. I knew I believed in him, but it was as though I wanted to prove "why" to myself, and to others. I have that kind of scientific mind. But God can't be proved by classical science. There's no experiment that proves God. So, in the end, I accepted that there are enough pointers in the physical world that prove God exists in the spiritual domain.'

'What do you mean?' I asked.

'Well, the wonder of the universe, for one. Then there are the testimonies of other believers. In the end, I just had to take a mental step of faith.'

We sat for a while, dwelling on what Mike had said. I really admired the strength of his story. 'I guess I've never been aware of God working great and marvellous miracles in my life,' he finished, quietly. 'But I do know that he's been guiding, directing and blessing me every step of the way.'

'Amen, to that,' I said, with a reassuring smile.

The church was a big part of my life, but I needed to earn a living. During the day, I took on any kind of work to help pay the bills and save some money. Finding a job was sometimes a struggle, but I was never without one for long. I waited on tables, did painting and decorating and all manner of other jobs. Eventually, I found myself steady employment with a security company. It would have been easy for me to go back into close protection, but that was too close for comfort to my old life. Being a security guard was a waste of my skills in some ways and the pay was lousy, but I enjoyed the work and it was relatively peaceful. It took me to Kew Gardens and other tourist sights around London. It didn't really matter to me how I earned a living. My driving force was Jesus, and telling others about the new life he had given me. I prayed for opportunities to speak to people. Many came my way.

It wasn't long, however, before the security company

realised the weight of my past work record in close protection. Promotion was offered and I quickly rose up through the ranks. I liked being good at what I did and I knew I could make big improvements in the way things were being managed. Without realising, I soon grew quietly ambitious. A couple of years went by and I changed jobs within the business, each time securing a better package for myself. Before I knew it, I was a senior national accounts manager, with a company car, a fully-funded flat in central London and a respectable salary. I thanked God for what I believed was his provision. By then, Sara was a newly-qualified teacher and we began making plans to get married.

We spent many weekends at Sara's parents' home in Essex. I had a lot to prove to them. They were loving, accepting people, but I was very aware that I was hardly the kind of man they had in mind for their daughter. All I could do was pray that they would see the 'new me', the man that God was moulding and refining day by day.

It was not always easy. Though I had long since abandoned Kung Fu, it was still very much a part of me. One weekend I was enjoying an extended stay at their home. I planned to catch an early train into London on Monday morning. At about 5 a.m., David, Sara's father, decided to wake me up with a cup of tea. I was sleeping soundly. In a split second, my old, ingrained instincts took over. Someone was entering the room. Immediately alert and 'in defence', I vaulted up in a fighting horse position. Poor David hardly knew what was going on. I stopped myself just in time, before taking a strike at him. He did well to hold on to the cup of tea, as he leapt in surprise.

David often laughs about that incident but, to me, it is a painful reminder of the old 'way' that can never be truly erased from my being. Kung Fu will always be the 'thorn in my flesh.' Using pressure points on the body, I can kill a man in seconds. That kind of knowledge is dangerous. It's like walking around with a loaded gun. In the early days, Sara often told me she felt safe when we were out together. It wasn't what I wanted to hear.

From that incredible day when God demonstrated his power as I wrestled with Alcaponey, I have always discouraged people from pursuing any form of martial art. In the West it is mainly taught for fitness and self-defence, but it is rooted in spirituality that I believe is misleading and dangerous. The 'way' of Kung Fu is a very different path to the true way of Christ. It is a way that builds false confidence in self. Martial arts appeal to a person's fears, weaknesses and ego. Christ's way is to release a person into new life, freedom and security through, and in, him.

Chapter 14

Sara and I married on 22 July 1995. Earlier that year, Sara's best friend, Helen, married Mike. Sadly, it meant both Mike and I left the Oak Room church within a few months of each other. Sara and Helen were both working in Essex, close to their family homes. The girls had been friends since childhood and both their families were members of Moorcroft Hall, a small local church.

We quickly became immersed in life at Moorcroft. From the early days of my conversion I imagined I would either go to China as a missionary, or work in prisons with hardened criminals. Instead, I found myself following Sara in her heart for children. Her father had led 'Searchlight' summer camps for years and I was amazed at how much I enjoyed getting involved with them. I loved playing games. It was something I had missed all my life. There were water fights and all manner of games and sports. In the evenings we shared the good news of Jesus Christ. It was easy. The kids were interested and I found they listened to me.

Moorcroft Hall had no outreach programme and hardly any young people. Before long, Mike, Helen, Sara and I decided to set up a youth club at the church. We knew there were many teenagers who had nothing better to do than hang around on the streets. We were a dynamic team. I played rough and Mike preached a good gospel message. Every Friday we drove a minibus around the Basildon area, picking up kids to take to the church hall. Many of them put their trust in Jesus Christ.

Jamie was a very troubled boy. He was 9 years old and very small for his age. He had a history of running away from home and getting into trouble. He trusted no one and stammered nervously as he talked. We never knew the full story of his background but, like many of the children we met, he came from a broken home and his mother struggled to care for him. We built relationships with as many parents as possible, always being truthful about the fact that I had been in prison. It carried very little stigma. Many of the women's husbands were also serving time and most of them appreciated our help in keeping their children off the streets.

Week after week, Jamie came along to the youth club. Very soon he brought his brother, John, and sister, Mandy. I often wonder how much worse Jamie's life might have become, had he not had our support in those precious days.

Becci Watson was a lovely young girl who we collected each week from Billericay. The club was growing and by now we needed a minibus and a couple of cars to pick up all the kids. One night I had just started the first game when I realised, to my horror, that I'd forgotten Becci.

Leaving the others to take over the game, I sped off, using all my protective driving skills, achieving the twenty-minute journey in a fraction of the time. Becci was still waiting. She was cold but forgiving. That was her nature. In the car we chatted, then I asked her straight out: 'So, Becci, do you believe in Jesus yet?' There was stunned silence. She had never been asked so directly. She stared straight ahead and I kept my eyes on the road. The silence remained until we pulled up in the church car park. I was unbuckling my seat belt and opening the door when Becci suddenly said, 'Yes.'

'Yes?' I queried.

'Yes, I believe in Jesus,' she said, looking me straight in the face. Her smile spread and her eyes twinkled. She repeated again, 'Yes, Tony. Now I believe in Jesus.' Becci has shared her testimony many times over the years. She always says she gave her life to Christ that night in my car. I was glad I'd had the guts to ask her such a direct question. Today, Becci is a natural evangelist who freely shares her faith and is an inspiration to me still.

There were many others who put their trust in Jesus and were hungry to learn more. Out of the Friday nights we set up a Tuesday evening Bible study group at our house. There wasn't a lot of room, but we regularly squeezed ten to fifteen young people in the living room. They were exciting days.

Meanwhile I was making good progress at work. There were promotions and salary increases and I was always looking ahead, chasing the next goal. My heart was still very much for the people in the world who did not know Jesus but, looking back now, I realise that my focus was being twisted. Sara and I deluded ourselves into thinking that God was providing all these good things for us, so that we could give more back to him. In reality that wasn't happening. My job became more demanding and often took me away from Sara, the church and the work I knew God was calling me to do. Without realising, I was becoming what I now call a 'comfortable Christian'.

Only a few years earlier I had been very scathing about the kind of person I had now become. When I first arrived in England I was eager to be part of a church. In prison, I had read about the early church in the New Testament and imagined what it would be like. It would be God's little treat for me. Sure enough, after spiritual survival in Cyprus it was a real prize to be among other believers. As time went by, however, I grew increasingly disillusioned with many churches I visited. Yes, the people might be loving, welcoming, enthusiastic and supportive of one another, but on the whole they were very tied up in their own lives. They prayed for the poor and needy, but few seemed willing to share their faith outside the church walls.

I read in my Bible, Mark 16:15, where Jesus tells his followers, 'Go into all the world and preach the good news to all creation.' It was a command of Jesus, meant as much for Christians today as for those in Bible times. Yet I didn't see many people doing it. I had been saved and transformed by Almighty God. It was inconceivable that I should not do everything in my power to persuade others of the truth about Jesus Christ. I imagined it was as though a man discovered the cure for cancer. Would he keep it from the rest of mankind? No. Yet how much more had I found? It was a matter of urgency to tell the world and I just couldn't fathom why so few others seemed to feel the same.

Six or seven years on, I, too, was caught up in the trappings of the good life. I had entered a spiritual wilderness, without even realising. There were trying times ahead.

By the summer of 1999, Mike and Helen had moved around the other side of the M25, to Berkshire, where Mike had been offered a good job. The youth group was still going strong, but Sara and I were frustrated by our church life. We were the only people of our age at Moorcroft Hall and we longed for more meaningful fellowship. God understood our discontent, we were sure. Indeed, we praised him for answered prayer when I was offered a job in Feltham. It meant more money and we could afford a nice house in a better area.

How foolish we were. Looking back now I see that God's provision was not a big salary and a nice house.

These things were nothing more than the trappings of a comfortable life. God's provision was the people we were already ministering to in Essex. The kids needed us and we walked out on them. Yes, we set each one up in a local church and ensured they were cared for, but ultimately we were following our way, not God's. If only we had realised that at the time.

A few weeks before moving house I was made redundant. 'What was God's plan in this?' I wondered. Still, I had built up a good C.V. and I knew it wouldn't be long before we were on our feet again. Within a few months, I secured an even better job as Marketing Director for a security company in central London. Soon after that we found out Sara was expecting our first baby. Life seemed good. We were convinced we were in the right place.

I took on the role of youth worker at the local evangelical church and set about establishing a youth group for the local teenagers. It wasn't without struggle. I faced frustrating battles with some of the church members. 'I think they're just worried that more people will wear out the pile on the carpet,' I joked sarcastically to Sara. I vowed that I would go on. I would shame them into action by showing them just what could, and what should, be done. In a few short months there was a thriving youth club.

Sure enough, through the youth club, many young people who had left the church were now coming back and bringing their friends. The rest of the members began to take notice. But still, there was so little passion for evangelism. Undeterred, I went ahead, like a bull in a china shop. Evangelism was Jesus' command and I would do it, with or without them. I had much to learn. God was about to pull the plug.

One Monday evening in early March 2000, one of the young boys in the youth group came to our house. I talked and prayed with him about some of the difficulties he was having at school and later in the evening I drove him home. On the way back from his house I decided to pick up a Chinese takeaway. It had been a long day and I was tired.

The windscreen showed a light pitter-patter of rain. It was dark and I drove carefully. In the past few months I'd had a couple of minor road accidents. I'd been pushing myself too hard, driving for my job, then again, taxiing the kids around in the evenings. The tiredness was beginning to get to me.

I was driving along an unlit country road. At that time of year there were always lots of deer around. 'Watch your speed,' I reminded myself. The last thing I wanted was a great stag leaping out in front of me.

Somehow I must have missed the warning stop sign. Before I realised it, I was at the crossroads. The red sign loomed large in front of me and I slammed on my brakes. The wheels locked. The car kept moving forwards. Thankfully, the main road was clear. There were no lights and no sign of any vehicles. The car skidded across to the other side of the road. What was that? As I drew to a halt, I felt something clip the front right hand side of the car. It was just a very small tap, but it was enough to flood me with panic. It must have been an animal. I got out to take a look. The headlight was broken, but there was no sign of anything else. I scanned the road behind. Maybe it had been a small deer or a fox that had limped back into the undergrowth.

Getting back in the car, I reversed a few metres, back to the crossroads. There was still nothing to see, but I had a strange sense of panic. I sat for a moment, gripping the steering wheel. Two other cars pulled up, a little distance from the junction. No one got out. 'Maybe they were stopped by the same animal,' I reasoned. I didn't know what to do. The food was getting cold. I was angry at myself for yet another foolish driving mistake. I didn't want to have to explain it to anyone. I especially didn't want to have to deal with an injured animal. Putting my foot down, I drove away, taking another route home. I thought nothing more of it.

The following Saturday some of the older kids from the youth group came to our house for lunch and a Bible study. One by one they filed into the living room. 'Hey Tony, what happened to the car?' asked Tom, mock punching me as he plonked himself down on a chair. Tom was heavily into radio communications and police activity. He was always tuning into the police frequencies and digging up newspaper reports on detective work. 'Y'know the police are looking for a car like yours,' he laughed.

'Oh yeah?' I queried, suddenly interested.

'There was a hit and run accident on Monday night and a lady was killed.' As he was talking, my blood ran cold.

'Where was that then?' I asked, trying to sound casual.

'On the Bracknell road. This woman was knocked off her motorbike. The driver didn't even stop.' I felt sick. What could I say? 'Well, you better hand me in then,' I joked, but inside I was dying. I couldn't get the kids out of the house fast enough.

'What's wrong with you?' asked Sara, irritably, as we waved the last one goodbye. 'I've never known you do a study so quickly.' I sat down on the settee with my head in my hands. Sara was suddenly worried. 'Hey, what is it. Are you ill?' she said. 'I've got to tell you something,' I replied, shaking, with tears of panic welling up in my eyes. I told Sara about the accident, how I thought I'd hit an animal and what Tom had said about a woman being killed.

'But how do you know it was the same accident?' said Sara, trying to stay calm.

'It had to be. It was the same time, the same place. Who else could it be?'

'Why didn't you tell me about it?

'Because I didn't think anything serious had happened.'

'But you must have felt the car hit someone?'

'It was hardly anything. Just a small tap. I thought it was an animal. See for yourself, there's only a bit of damage to the car.'

'So what are we going to do?' Sara asked, becoming choked. She, too, was now panicking.

I began pacing the room, trying to think. 'We can't do anything until we know for sure, can we?' I said. Sara was rifling through a pile of unread newspapers. Suddenly she clapped her hand to her mouth.

'No!' I grabbed the paper. It was all there in black and white. A lady on a motorbike had passed the junction at around 9.30 p.m. on Monday night. She had been knocked into the bushes, where she later died. She was a mother and a local scout troop leader. That night she had been travelling home after a meeting. The newspaper reported that the driver had sped off and that detectives were still looking to identify the vehicle.

I shook uncontrollably. Sara wept and held her stomach, as if to protect our unborn baby. 'If I have killed this lady, that means a jail sentence,' I said.

'But it was an accident, a stupid, stupid accident,' said Sara.

'A woman is dead,' I snapped. 'Accident or no accident, I will still go to jail.'

'But what about the baby?' Sara sobbed. 'What will we do?' We talked on into the night, reasoning that it could not be God's will for me to go back to prison, especially not now. Surely he would protect us from this? We prayed together, 'Lord Jesus, protect us, save us.' We pleaded with God, but they were pathetic prayers. We were demanding that he do our will, not his. We were wrong and heaven was silent.

We made the decision to do nothing.

A few days later we took the car to be fixed. I lied to the mechanics, saying I'd found it damaged in a car park. The garage gave me a replacement car until the repair could be done and I dropped Sara off at the school where she was teaching. As I began to drive away, terror gripped me. In the rear view mirror a policeman had pulled up on his bicycle and was talking to Sara. I stopped the car and went back. I was probably more panicked than Sara. She knew the policeman. His little boy was in her class.

'What happened to your car? He was asking her as I drew up alongside them. Sara looked at me anxiously.

'It's in the garage being serviced,' I said.

'Fine,' he smiled. 'It's just that we're on the look out for a car like yours. There are around five hundred of them registered in the area. One of them was involved in a hit and run accident the other week.' I was willing Sara to stay composed, whilst feeling violent rushes of sickness inside. Thankfully, the policeman soon rode away.

Immediately, I went back home and dug out the Yellow Pages. I knew I was in deep trouble. We needed a solicitor.

Very early the next morning there was a loud knock at the door. I leapt out of bed and ran downstairs. Half a dozen policemen with dogs barged in as I opened the door. Sara appeared at the top of the stairs, looking frightened and pale. They placed us both under arrest and began searching the house, rifling through our rubbish bins and unplugging the computer to take away.

Sara remained silent. The neighbours' curtains twitched as the police bundled us into separate cars. I felt sick to the core. How could I have got us into this? How would Sara handle it? Once at the police station, we were kept apart and led into individual interview rooms. We couldn't tell our story fast enough. No more lies. We were both desperate to spill out the details of this dreadful accident. I couldn't care less about the interrogation. I wanted to die. All I could think about was the woman I had killed. As an evangelist I was in the business of leading people to Jesus to receive new life. Now I had caused the untimely death of an innocent lady. Like me, she had been travelling home from doing youth work. She had two children at home. What if she was not a Christian? I had taken away her chance of eternal life. I pleaded with God that he would give her my place in heaven and send me to the depths of hell. I would have given my life there and then if I could have brought her back. I longed for God to strike me down.

The police were sympathetic. They realised the truth of the situation. Forensic evidence proved I was travelling well below the speed limit, but the roads were wet and the lady had no lights on her motorbike. That was little comfort to me. I had still taken a life and ruined a family.

'All this had nothing to do with Sara,' I pleaded with them. 'Please, let her go.' I knew Sara wouldn't be able to handle the situation. She had been arrested because the car was registered in her name. The police no doubt thought it would help get a full confession out of me.

'Look, this is a straightforward accident,' said the sergeant, trying to be reassuring. 'All the evidence proves that. The Crown Prosecution Service will be lenient.' I shook my head in despair. I didn't care about that. I deserved to be punished. 'If this woman hadn't been killed, there wouldn't even be a case,' the sergeant continued. 'The most you'll get from this will be a driving ban.'

The weeks and months ahead were hellish. It was hard to talk to people about what had happened. We couldn't bear to keep going through the story. Even our closest friends knew only some of what was going on. The hardest blow was from the church. We had been honest with them but, at a time when we desperately needed their love and support, it was as though they turned their back on us. They put a 'caretaker' youth worker in my place to continue the work I had been doing. It felt like a kick in the teeth. I grappled hard to understand their decision, but it was a deep and painful struggle.

Each day seemed more stressful than the last. In the midst of it, on 11 June 2000, Sara gave birth to a baby boy we named Ethan. It should have been the most joyous occasion of my life, but it was clouded in anxiety. What if I ended up being sent back to prison? How would Sara cope alone with the baby? How could I provide for them?

We persevered for almost six more months, before deciding to leave the area. We found a house in Didcot, but we didn't stay there long either. With a new baby, Sara wanted to be nearer to her parents. We moved back to Essex and I took on a role as youth pastor with a homeless organisation in Southend. The director, Ron Wright, showed good faith in me. He knew my situation, but immediately recognised my heart for evangelism and passion to help young people. Ron probably suspected that, being somewhat messed up myself, I could relate well to the troubled homeless kids he was dealing with.

In the meantime, Sara and I found ourselves on our knees before God. It was the beginning of a long, painful learning process, out of which we grew immensely in our relationship with him and with each other. Sara tells her own story about this time. Mine was an ongoing lesson in brokenness, humility and grace. I realised that, for years I had been storming ahead, driven by my passion to share the gospel, but working very much on my own agenda. I had not allowed God the space to use me as he wanted. I had been arrogant in my evangelistic work and judgemental of others who I believed were failing God. Only now was I beginning to realise the error of my ways. For the first time in our relationship, Sara and I began praying earnestly together. Our prayers changed. No longer were they selfish pleas that God would do our will. Now, we were placing ourselves totally in his hands and asking him to give us the grace to accept his plan and purpose. Despite Sara's many years of faith and all my dramatic experiences of God, we both felt we were very much on the bottom rung of the ladder in our relationship with him.

Each month seemed to bring a legal meeting or some new development in our case. We liaised regularly with our barristers. Sara found the meetings especially difficult. It came as no surprise to me, but she was shocked at the wheeling and dealing of the justice system. People involved were obviously lying and our barristers were encouraging us to say things that weren't strictly true, to help our case. From defence to prosecution, everyone was bound up in plea bargaining and negotiating.

'Why can't we just tell the truth?' Sara pleaded with her barrister. He smiled weakly at her naivety. 'Whichever way we turn, we're committing sin,' she said desperately, looking at me. I didn't know what to do. I hated the system as much as she did.

'Tell me again,' I said to my barrister, 'what exactly am I being charged with?'

'The charge is death by careless driving and perverting the course of justice,' he told me. 'That's because of your lie to the policeman,' he said. 'They'll probably also add the charge of failing to stop and report an accident, but it's fairly weak.' I wrung my hands in frustration. 'It's a good charge, Tony, the best we could hope for,' he said. 'It won't carry a prison sentence. At least you're not up for death by dangerous driving.'

'And what about Sara?' I asked. The two men conferred together, then Sara's barrister spoke. 'If you admit to lying to the policeman, it will get her off the hook. I'm sure there'll be no charge.'

'But that's the truth, anyway,' I said in despair. 'It was me who lied. Sara never said a word,' I implored. The barristers consulted their notes. 'It appears the policeman has given evidence to the contrary,' one of them said. 'He claims it was Sara who lied to him about where the car was that morning.' Sara bit her bottom lip. The barrister patted her hand. 'Don't worry, I don't think this will stand up in court. You have a clean record so there shouldn't be any problem.' We sat in silence for a few moments.

'Tony, there is something else,' the other barrister said, slowly. 'It might not be taken into account, but you need to be prepared.' I knew what was coming. I was still living with the shock and shame of an incident only a few weeks earlier.

I had been asked by one of my company's top clients to arrange a meeting over a meal at a Greek restaurant in London. When I telephoned to make a booking I was confronted with a rude, arrogant man. 'I'd like to make a reservation for six people tomorrow evening,' I said. 'Do you have any vacancies?'

'Of course we've got vacancies,' came the reply, 'we are a restaurant, what do you think?' I was quite taken aback by his attitude, but I continued. 'I will be entertaining a very important client,' I told him. 'Can you reserve me a good table?'

'They are all good tables,' he snapped. 'Malagas!' he muttered under his breath.

'What did you say?'

'I said they are all good tables here.'

'I heard exactly what you said. I speak Greek, you Malagas, I know what you just called me.'

'Ah, you bloody idiot, you bother me with these stupid questions, I don't need you here,' he said, in a heated temper.

Disbelief gave way to seething anger. A rage boiled up inside me. I let out a torrid stream of abuse in Greek. The lid flew off my pent-up stress. Despite all the years of freedom, it was as though I was the old Tony again. I called him every rude and insulting name under the sun. All the tension of the months since the accident came pouring out in my anger. Finally, I slammed the phone down. Instantly, it rang back. I snapped it up. It was him. Another stream of abuse. He put the phone down. Immediately, I called him again, fury raging within me. This time he hung up straight away. The next call I took was from the police. He had reported me.

My barrister handed me a document. 'You're being charged with harassment on this one, Tony.' I was sick and ashamed and hardly dare look at Sara. 'I know you'll think this is stupid, but a charge like this carries more weight than anything to do with the accident.' I kicked my chair back and stood up. This was all so very, very wrong. Again, all I could think about was the poor woman I had killed and the family I had broken.

We were called to court in early June 2001. Before entering the courtroom Sara and I attended a short briefing with our advisers. They were both confident, but I felt sick and irritated. 'Don't worry,' my barrister stressed. 'It's looking good. The CPS (Crown Prosecution Service) are promising there won't be anything more than a driving ban and some sort of community service, if not a suspended sentence.'

We sat in the dock, listening to our case. After an hour the judge began to sum up, but there was much conferring between him and the barristers. I was concerned. What was going on? Eventually, he announced that more time was needed to examine the complexities of my case and that my sentencing would be postponed. I glanced at Sara. She looked as confused as I felt. She smiled weakly and squeezed my hand. She was pale and tired. What was I putting her through?

'Sara Anthony, please rise,' said the judge. Sara stood up and I noticed her skirt slightly moving as her legs quivered. I held my breath. The judge began speaking, telling her that she had been wrong not to report the incident as soon as she knew about it. She nodded, standing straight and strong, but I could see the white of her knuckles as she clung to the dock. I had a horrible sinking feeling. 'You are ordered to do 120 hours' community service,' the judge finished. 'Please sit down.'

Sara sank back onto her chair, tears welling up in her eyes. She managed to stay in control, as I battled internally with anger and confusion. I looked accusingly at her barrister. He shook his head, as if in disbelief.

I was called back to court on 29 June. Since Sara had already received her sentence, she was obliged to stay behind the frosted glass of the public gallery. I stood alone in the dock. I stared towards the glass. Her being there was a support. Suddenly a face peered around the side of the partition. I had seen him before. He had been at every hearing. He was a young guy, around 18 years old, with short dark hair and sunken eyes. He glared at me. I looked away and swallowed hard. Was it her son? Was this the boy I had deprived of a mother? He disappeared, back behind the glass. Then there was a girl's face. I couldn't bear to look. Sickness ran over me in waves. If my barrister was correct, I would walk out of here a free man, but I would never have any peace. The boy's face would stay with me forever.

The case began and the lawyers seemed to cover much old ground. It had all been said before. My barrister's defence completely galled me. He was only doing his job, but I hated the way he made me sound like an innocent victim, being wrongly persecuted. I thought about the family behind the glass. No one would ever understand the true weight of my guilt and internal torment. Next, the barrister for the Crown Prosecution began his case. This time he referred to my Interpol record and the fact that I had been in prison before. Immediately, my barrister objected. 'That is nothing to do with this charge, my Lord,' he said. He was told to sit down.

The case went on. After a while I was hardly listening. It all seemed irrelevant. I was guilty before God and I wanted to die. When the sentence finally came there were several gasps in the courtroom.

Fifteen months' imprisonment.

Chapter 15

The blacked out police van sped through the Oxfordshire countryside. My hands were cuffed and I sat hugging my knees in a small caged cubicle. Shame and remorse rained down on me in torrents. What had I become? What would Michael Wright think if he could see me now?

The words of a song rang in my head. It was the hymn, *And Can It Be?* I dwelt on one of the verses: 'Long my imprisoned spirit lay, fast bound in sin and nature's night . . . ' I thought of the times I had sung the hymn with a grateful heart. It was so much my story:

> And can it be that I should gain
> An interest in the Saviour's blood?
> Died he for me, who caused His pain –
> For me, who Him to death pursued?
> Amazing love! How can it be,
> That thou, my God, shouldst die for me?

The truth of the hymn cut me to the core. Tears began streaming down my cheeks. I thought back over my life. I was a wicked man who God had saved. How little I deserved him. Now it was as though I had ripped the heart out of my story, the one I had told so many times to convince others of the truth about Jesus Christ. How could I ever expect God to use me again? I vowed, there and then, to become a quiet Christian. I could never give up on God. He was too real to me. But I was not worthy to have Jesus' name on my lips.

Looking up, the other prisoner caught my eye. There were only two of us in the van. He was a young man, with a large ring in his eyebrow and a shaven head. He smiled at me. It was a smile that said, 'Don't worry mate, you'll get through it.' He had no idea. Prison wouldn't bother me. I could handle myself in jail. After Nicosia, HMP Bullingdon would be easy. My prison was inside my head. The bars were wrapped around my heart, suffocating me in shame. It was the worst time in my life.

HMP Bullingdon, home for the next eight months, minimum. I went through the motions quietly. Body search, photograph, fingerprints. It was all too familiar. At least Bullingdon was light and airy, nothing like Nicosia's dungeon.

I was put in a cell with two other men. As the officers showed me in, the inmates immediately set about them, moaning and cursing. 'This place is the pits man,' one spat. 'When are we getting our TV? It was promised two weeks ago!'

They sickened me. Where did they think they were, a holiday camp? This wasn't prison. Compared to Nicosia, this was like kindergarten. Walking through the block I'd passed men playing snooker and table tennis. There were computers, televisions and all manner of facilities. I climbed onto my bunk. It was far from comfortable, but at least there was a mattress and blankets, and it was vaguely clean.

I hardly dared think about Sara and Ethan. Sara must hate me now. I hated myself for what I'd done to her. What kind of husband was I? What kind of father could I ever be? I'd probably damaged our son forever.

Sara began writing to me almost every day. She sent in my Bible and a few other books. Her letters were encouraging, but I often wished, for her sake, that we had never met. Sara was doing her community service working in a local charity shop. It must have been a struggle with the baby, but she didn't complain. She and Ethan had moved in with her parents but she was looking for a flat. It wasn't easy. With me in prison there were good state benefits, but everything in the area was way beyond her reach. I remembered some of the families we'd worked with in those early days in Essex and dreaded that she'd end up the same, in some squalid bedsit.

As the weeks went by, I kept myself to myself. My apparent 'good behaviour' earned me a cell to myself. I relished the relative peace. Bullingdon was never quiet. It got to you after a while. The worst time was when the NONCE (Not Of Normal Criminal Explanation) wing was released into the main block. It happened a couple of times a week. All other prisoners were locked in their cells. The NONCEs were the most hated of all men in the prison. They were the paedophiles and child abusers. The noise was deafening. Inmates banged on their cell doors, yelling abuse and smashing anything they could to make the biggest disturbance, showing their disgust and hatred.

'What I wouldn't give for a few moments alone with one of those freaks,' said Lenny, slapping his fist into his palm.

'I'm sure people have said that about me in the past,' I said.

'Ah no, you're not like them, they're sick, evil,' said Lenny, aggressively punching the air as he walked away.

'Like I said.'

I agreed with Lenny. When I thought about these men, and my own young son, my flesh crawled. I could understand the hatred towards them. But then, were they really any worse than me, or any of the other men?

It was hard to come to terms with, but I knew what the Bible taught about sin: no one is perfect, all have fallen short of God's standard. I remembered Michael Wright likening sin to black ink on a white shirt. The smallest white lie might be a tiny black spot on the shirt, but it is enough to ruin it. When the shirt is put in water, the ink spreads, leaving it a dirty grey colour. I thought about my own life. There were great big black blotches all over my shirt!

Staring out through the bars, I reflected back to my time in Cyprus and to some of Michael's teaching. 'The world doesn't know how to handle sin,' I remembered him saying. He'd gestured to the other prisoners in the visiting room. 'We try to grade and measure sin and we lock up those who we think are worse than us.' He'd leaned forward and spoken more quietly, 'Society hides its ugliness in institutions to make itself look more righteous, Tony,' he'd said, 'but to God, there is no difference when it comes to sin.'

'I suppose that's the way the authorities and the outside world look at us lot in here,' I'd told him. 'We're all as bad and as mad as one another.'

'Precisely. And that's the way we all are before God. Every one of us, whether we're locked up for our wrongdoing or not, we're all tainted by sin in God's eyes, so we're all separated from him.'

'But then came Jesus?'

'You got it,' Michael had smiled. 'Jesus tackled sin head on. When he died on the cross he took on the full weight of the world's sin: past, present and future. Because of Jesus we can all be forgiven. We don't need to pay for our sins, or serve the sentence we deserve. Jesus has already done that.'

I smiled as I remembered Michael, animated and excited as he spilled out these words in his Irish lilt.

'That's why you're as free a man today as I am, Tony,' he'd grinned, knowing that I understood exactly what he meant.

Everything seemed to make so much sense back then. Crazy, but it was easier to be a Christian in Nicosia than it was in the outside world. All I wanted to do was tell other people what I'd found. Where had it gone so wrong?

One day I was reading my Bible in my cell when Darren Brown walked in. He was the guy who had travelled into Bullingdon with me that first day. Quickly, I stuffed the Bible under my pillow. 'What ya reading?' he asked.

'Nothing much,' I said defensively. I didn't want to get into conversation. Darren slumped down on the bed, slouching against the wall.

'What d'ya mean, nothing much?' he said. 'Is it a dirty book or something?'

I was irritated. 'Actually I'm reading my Bible,' I snapped rudely.

'A Bible? What, are you religious then, one of them Christians or something?'

'Well, I'm not much of a Christian am I? I'm in prison.'

'Hey, everyone makes mistakes, mate.'

'Yeah, but I should have known better.'

'So what are you reading in the Bible. Is it interesting?' Darren continued to question. I grew more irritated. Why couldn't he just leave me alone?

'What does it matter?' I came back at him. 'I don't really want to talk about it, y'know.'

'Alright, keep your hair on. I was just asking a question,' he said, raising both hands up in defence. I realised how rude I was being.

'OK,' I said, reluctantly, 'I was reading my favourite verse in John 8:36, about Jesus setting me free.' My tone was still aggressive and Darren had clearly had enough. He got up.

'Come and play ping pong when you've calmed down, eh mate?' He walked out and I wrung my hands in frustration. Being a Christian was the last thing I wanted to talk about.

Three days later, Darren visited me again. Now he perched on the end of the bed, smiling all over his face. 'You'll never guess what, mate?'

'What?' I laughed. His mischievous grin was infectious. 'I got into so much trouble after I left you the other day.'

'Why what happened?'

'I went to the chapel to get a Bible. You were so cagey about what you were reading, I wanted to read it myself,' he said. I slowly rubbed my face into my hands, wondering what was coming next. Darren continued, 'I asked the chaplain for a Bible. He probably thought I was going to use the pages to make roll-ups. He wouldn't give me one so, when he wasn't looking, I nicked one anyway. I shoved it up my jumper.'

'Don't tell me, you got caught.'

'Yep, they searched me and found it and locked me in solitary for twenty-four hours.'

'No way!'

'What they didn't find was the other one I'd shoved down my pants,' Darren said, his eyes twinkling. I couldn't help but laugh. 'Well, it gave me something to do while I was locked up,' he continued. 'I wanted to find the bit you'd said about, but I had no idea where it was. I thought you'd said something about James or John or Jack, but I've never opened a Bible before.'

'It's in the Gospel of John,' I said weakly.

'I know that now,' he beamed. 'I banged on the wall to the guy in the cell next door, "Hey mate, d'ya know anything about the Bible?" He came back, "Yeah, I'm a Christian, what d'ya wanna know?" I told him what you'd said about Jesus setting you free and he suggested I tried the Gospel of John.' Darren continued, 'I found it in the index and started to read from the beginning. I had nothing else to do, did I?' he laughed. 'At first I didn't understand it at all, Tony. All that stuff about the Word being God and being made flesh. It was nonsense to me. But after that it just tells you all about what Jesus did. Water into wine, and that Samaritan bird at the well, how he knew what a slapper she was. It gets really interesting doesn't it?'

'Yes,' I agreed quietly, 'it gets really interesting.'

'So I read the whole book. I got to that part you said about. I can remember it, "if the Son sets you free, you will be free indeed." I read on and on, then I came back to that bit again.' Darren quietened now, looking for my response. 'I think I get it, mate. I really get it,' he said. 'I read about Jesus and I believe in him. I even tried to talk to him last night. Does that mean I'm a Christian?'

I sat, transfixed in shock and amazement. I had done everything possible to put Darren off. But God showed me he was going to use me, despite my best efforts. It was as though he was saying to me, 'Now I will really use you. Now you are broken and weak, I can work my will through you.'

'Are you crying, mate?' Darren's voice broke into my thoughts. I hastily wiped my wet eyes. I hardly knew what to say to him, but he was anxious to talk. We spoke until 'bang up' time, Darren spilling out his story. He was an orphan. He had been passed from foster family to foster family and had been in trouble with the police all his adult life. Prison was no big deal. He'd served time before. This time it was because he had found his girlfriend being chatted up by another man. He had slashed the man's face with a bottle. 'I lost her after that,' he told me, 'I think she's with him now.'

'Then let's pray about it,' I said.

Darren was nervous. He found it hard to pray with me. 'I don't know how to,' he said. I bowed my head and talked to God, just as Darren had been talking to me. After that, Darren and I got together most days. He often asked me to pray with him and I began preparing Bible studies, the way I had for my friends in Nicosia.

Life wasn't easy for Darren. He was hooked on drugs. It was easy to get them inside. Everyone was given regular tests and huge numbers of men lost their remission or were punished for testing positive. It was just a way of life. Darren really struggled. Cannabis had fried his brain. He'd started smoking when he was a teenager and now he suffered from depression and paranoia. I tried to counsel him, to keep him away from the suppliers and to pray with him about it. Sometimes he stayed clean for weeks at a time, which was a huge achievement. I was desperate to help Darren. He was the man who'd led me back to a right relationship with God.

Through that first experience with him, I learned that I had no right to keep the gospel to myself. I had to let God use me. More than that, I learned it all had to be in his timing. No more bullish Tony-style evangelism. No more arrogance. No more belting ahead in my own strength. I had to be down on my hands and knees and face, utterly broken before God. My prayer life was to change, radically. I realised that I'd never had much time for prayer before. I'd always been too busy, just being busy. My prayers had been little more than on-the-run lists of requests about what I needed God to do. Ironically, all that time, God had simply wanted me to slow down and be in his presence. Now I knew what I needed, most of all, was to spend time listening to him.

Breaking the blade out of my Gillette, I cut a piece of paper into the shape of a cross. On it I drew a mountain scene with streams and grass and trees. Using toothpaste, I stuck it in the middle of my window. My cell was on the ground floor, looking out over the courtyard where the men exercised. I kept my cell immaculately tidy and clean. It was a quiet and simple way to witness. I made sure I shared everything I had and was open and friendly with everyone.

Slowly, men began seeking me out, wanting to talk. It was easy to share my story with them, and with the officers and wardens I came to know. Many were surprised when they heard how I'd ended up in Bullingdon. They couldn't understand why an accident like mine carried a prison sentence. I was often referred to as an 'innocent man'. It gave me lots of opportunity to talk about my capacity to make mistakes, even though I was a Christian. 'I believe I should be here,' I would say. 'God is allowing me this experience to teach me things.' Very soon I was given the nickname 'Pastor', or sometimes 'Hope Dealer' (as opposed to many more 'dope dealers' in the prison!).

Every day, in my forty minutes' exercise in the courtyard, I found myself sharing the gospel. One time, Nigel Peters, a man serving a life sentence for murder, caught up with me. He was a bald, clean-shaven man in his mid-forties. He never smoked and kept himself fit by walking. We paced heavily together, each sharing our stories. 'I've noticed you're different to the others,' he said. 'Everyone else boasts about their crimes. All I hear you talk about is God.' I smiled at him and continued walking.

A couple of days later, I bumped into Nigel coming out of the gym. Sweat poured off him. 'Good workout?' I asked.

'To tell you the truth, I'm sick of it all,' he replied. I could tell he was depressed and upset. 'I've served over fourteen years now, Tony. Kept my nose clean the whole time. Now look at me, back in this place.' Nigel had only recently been transferred to Bullingdon from a more open prison. He'd earned himself a day release, but then it had all gone wrong. There had been some trouble with drug users on his block. 'I just lost it with them one night,' he told me. 'I went mad. It landed me in here. No chance of day release till the end of my sentence, another three and a half years.' We walked in silence for a while.

Suddenly, out of the blue, he asked, 'How can there be a God, Tony, when this kind of thing happens?' I thought for a while, then asked, 'Can I tell you a story?'

'Go on then.'

'There was once a shipwreck, with just one survivor. He made it to a desert island, but when he got there he realised what a desperate situation he was in. He prayed feverishly to God, but nothing happened.'

'That'd be right,' Nigel interrupted.

'All he could do was build a hut to protect himself from the elements,' I continued. 'One day he returned to the hut after scavenging for food, only to find that the hut was on fire. The midday sun had set it alight and he watched as his last hope went up in smoke. He was angry. "How can God allow such a thing?" he cried. That night he lay under a tree, scared and cold. In the morning he was woken up by rescuers. "How did you find me?" he asked them in amazement. "We saw your smoke signals," they said.'

Nigel sniffed dismissively as I finished the story. 'Sometimes God's love can feel like hatred,' I said. 'We don't always understand why he allows certain things in our lives. I couldn't understand why he was letting this happen to me,' I said. 'And you, losing your privileges like that. I imagine that feels like your last hope going up in smoke.'

'Too right,' Nigel said.

'But listen,' I continued. 'There's a verse in the Bible, in the book of Romans, chapter 8 verse 28. It says that in all things God works for the good of those who love him. The key word in that, Nigel, is *all*. It means everything, the good, the bad, you losing your open conditions . . . If you place your trust in Jesus Christ, even in such a situation as this, you won't be defeated. Look at this as a triumph. Through this situation, right now, God is working for your good.'

Nigel stopped. I could sense I was really getting through to him. 'He loves you, Nigel, he cares for you like you're his own child.'

He looked at me. 'Thank you for the story,' he said and slowly walked away.

The next day Nigel caught up with me again in the courtyard. 'Tony, that story you told me hasn't left my head,' he said. 'I can't get it out of my mind. Tell me more about your God.'

I shared the gospel with him, but I knew I had to go beyond the news of salvation. I'd learned only too well the difficulties of the Christian life. 'God will not save you from suffering,' I told him. 'It's in the times of suffering that he can do his best work in you. I know myself how little I rely on him when my life is going well. I'm learning that lesson the hard way, Nigel, but every day I thank God that he has brought me here and taught me these things.'

'But I'm not sure I have the faith, Tony.'

'Oh you have faith, my friend,' I replied. 'Think about when you woke up this morning. You breathed. You didn't think twice about whether there was oxygen. I can't see it here now, can you?' He smiled and I continued, 'The last time you sat down on a chair, did you pick it up and examine it to check whether it would hold you? No you didn't.' Now he laughed. 'That's the way it is with God,' I said, looking into his eyes. 'He *is* here, you just have to believe it.' Nigel looked away, gazing up into the sky.

'Once there was a boy,' I told him, 'flying his kite. It was a foggy day and his grandfather came up and said to him, "What are you doing?" The boy replied, "I'm flying my kite." The grandfather teased him, "I see no kite up there." The boy looked up and he couldn't see it either. He thought for a while, then he said to his grandfather, "but I know it's there. I can feel the tug on the string."'

I turned to him. 'Nigel, if you have faith in Jesus, you'll feel his tug in your heart.'

That night I wrote to Nigel. I outlined again what I'd said to him, backing it up with verses from the Bible and giving him passages to read that I knew would help him. It wasn't long before he came to a real and strong faith in Jesus. Soon after my release from Bullingdon he was transferred to a prison in Chelmsford, where I still visit him today.

Two of the toughest men on the block were Bulla and Ferguson. Soon, they, too, were walking the courtyard in my company. Bulla was from London's East End. Built like a heavyweight boxer, he had no neck and his massive shoulders supported arms thicker than most men's thighs. He was a debt collector, serving time for racially inspired violence. All his family were ardent fascists. That was the way he was raised.

Nobody messed with Bulla. He was big trouble, especially for the blacks or anyone who was of mixed race.

One of the officers obviously thought he'd prevent a situation by spilling some of my details to him. Prison records are supposed to be confidential, but officers often let information slip. They knew of my Kung Fu world title and my Interpol record. 'They might call him Pastor, but that guy is known around the world. He could break your neck with his bare hands,' the officer told Bulla.

Suddenly Bulla was interested. He seemed to set aside the fact that I was not pure-bred Caucasian. He wanted to know about Kung Fu. Rumours about my past spread like wildfire around the prison. It wasn't something I ever talked about much, but it earned me a certain respect, especially among the hard cases. I guess they were curious as to why a guy like me would share his Mars bars, help other prisoners write letters and pray with anyone who needed it.

'Yeah, I reckon I could do a bit of that Kung Fu myself,' Bulla joked with me one day as we walked in the yard. He started doing mock kicks and punches. 'And Buddha, yeah, I can see the appeal. Not that I'm religious, but I know it's a big deal to you. I might try a bit for myself one day, probably Buddhism or what's that chamanism thing? I suppose it's all the same at the end of the day, eh?'

I stopped walking and looked him straight in the face. 'No, you're missing the point, mate,' I said firmly. He was a little taken aback. 'What you're talking about is just religious soup, it means nothing, it's a deception. It will do nothing for you. It's all a lie.'

'Steady on, Tony.'

'No, listen to me. There's a big difference between having faith in God and following other religions of the world. I believe in one almighty creator God and his son, Jesus Christ. Only Jesus said, "I am the way and the truth and the life, no one comes to the Father, except through me."'

'Yeah, how arrogant is that!'

'It's not arrogant Bulla, it's the truth. The Bible tells us in 1 Corinthians 8:6 that there is only one God who gave us everything, and only one Lord, Jesus Christ. You can't argue with truth, or compromise it by mixing it up with rubbish from man-made religions.'

We started walking again, then Bulla piped up, 'I suppose it's like me with Millwall.'

'What do you mean?'

'Well, they're clearly the best team, right? The one and only. The champions.'

'Go on,' I said, wondering where this was leading.

'Well, it's whatever floats your boat, innit Tony? For you it's religion and this Jesus. For me it's Millwall football club.'

I felt like banging my head against the nearest wall, but I laughed along with him. 'No, no, you still don't get it . . .'

'What, get what?'

'Jesus isn't just a hobby to me, or my interest. It's not like I'm into Jesus the same way you're into football, or chess or ballroom dancing . . .'

'Watch it, mate!'

'Look, for me, Jesus is like oxygen. It's not just nice to have him in my life, he's essential to my life. He is life. Whether you accept that or not is your business, but it's still the truth. It's something I know and I'm desperate that everyone else finds out, too. It's life and death.'

'I can see that, you never shut up about it! It's alright for you, but it's only what you believe.'

'Me and millions of others who have taken that step of faith and realised the truth for themselves.'

'Yeah, but I'm not one of them.'

'OK, say you're in the pub with your mates watching a big football game. It comes to a free kick, but you're desperate for a pee. You leave quickly and in that time the kick is taken and your goalkeeper manages to save it. You rejoin your mates and they're ecstatic. They've seen the save. It's the best save they've ever seen. You're gutted that you missed it. But do you doubt it happened? No. You believe it, even though you didn't see it for yourself. You believe it because your mates can't shut up about it. You missed the best save ever, but they saw it, so now you're convinced, too.'

'I get what you're saying. Just because I haven't seen it, doesn't mean it isn't the truth. You're saying Jesus exists, it's just I haven't seen it for myself.'

'That's right. I'm telling you Jesus made the greatest save ever when he died for you, and me. I know it, because someone told me and now I believe it and have experienced its truth for myself. I'm going to be boasting about that save for the rest of my days.'

'Guess I'm still in the loo then?'

'No, Bulla, you came out of the loo when I first told you about Jesus. Now you just have to step up to the bar and accept your free pint.'

'Now you're talking.'

'Yep, it's there, already poured out for you,' I said with a smile. Bulla knew what I was saying. We had many similar conversations. I still pray that one day he'll come to accept the truth behind my stories.

Ferguson was another of the tough men. He was a black guy who rivalled Bulla in stature. He worked in the kitchens. One day he came up to me, 'Oi, Tony. I hear you're some sort of Christian.' I stopped in my tracks, imagining I was about to get a good kicking. Would I be able to take it gracefully?

'Yes, I am,' I said, trying not to show my fear. His response shocked me a little.

'My wife's just died,' he said. I braced myself mentally. So he was going to take his anger out on me. A few seconds went by. Then I felt his firm grip on my shoulder. 'Will you pray for her?' he asked. It took me a few moments to compose myself.

'Yes, I'll pray for her,' I said, 'and I'm also gonna pray for you cos you're the one left here.' We talked some more. He poured out his fears and worries about what would happen to his children. All I could do was pray with him and he accepted that gratefully.

After that, Ferguson gave me extra oranges and pudding whenever he was on serving duty.

One of the most sought after positions in the prison was that of 'Red Band'. At £5 a week, it was one of the best paid jobs. Red Bands were cleaners who were trusted to work, unsupervised, outside the prison block. The wardens were extremely vigilant when handing out this role. A high wall surrounded the perimeter of the prison, but if a man was determined and fit enough he could probably scale it without too much difficulty. For me, the job was a gift from God. It was a filthy task, but I relished being outside, alone, in the fresh air. Each day I used a shovel and a rake, filling nearly twenty large bin bags from one area alone. Bullingdon is a 'B' category, high security prison, but it's amazing what the men can get hold of. The block was on two floors, with two levels of windows from which they slung used needles, condoms, rotten fruit, bottles, newspapers and often toilet waste. Some of them behaved no better than animals.

There were those who resented my privilege. I would often have things hurled at me, everything from bottles to oranges or soap bars in socks, to hot water. Dodging the missiles wasn't always easy, but I prayed continually as I went along. After a while I came to know most of the men in the lower ground rooms. It wasn't long before I had shared the gospel in some way with each of them. In one room there were two Polish guys, Andrzej and Bolek. They were professional kidnappers, big, brutish men, serving long sentences. One of them spoke basic English, but it wasn't easy to communicate.

One night, I sat down to write them a letter, trying to explain the gospel in the most simple English I could. I also used Greek, thinking that their language shared some similarities. A couple of days later I was doing my rounds when Andrzej beckoned to me through the window. 'Thank you, Tony, for your letter. We did not realise,' he said, excitedly, 'you know Polish.'

'What?' I said, astonished.

'Your letter. It is very fluent. Perfect Polish,' Andrzej grinned. 'My friend here can understand. Thank you so much.' I didn't know what to say. Of all the languages of which I have a basic grasp, Polish is not one.

'No, no,' I said. 'I wrote in English and Greek.' Andrzej looked puzzled. He disappeared from the window, jabbering something in Polish. In the next moment, Bolek pushed him aside, greeting me eagerly with the letter in his hand.

'Yes, yes. Good Polish,' was all he could say, but he was grinning from ear to ear. I knew then that God had worked a miracle.

I praised him and prayed as I went about my work. When I had finished I rang the buzzer to be let back into the main block. Often the officers ignored me. I knew that they were allowing me time to sit down on the grass and read my Bible or gaze out to the hills beyond the prison wall.

One day a voice called out from one of the top floor cells. 'Oi, Pastor, Jesus is dead y'know?' I was instantly

upset. I'd had grief from this guy before. He'd thrown
bottles and hurled abuse, but I'd never seen his face. I
gripped the spade, thinking how much I'd like to shove
it through the man's head. Instead, I thought about what
Jesus would do and decided to ignore him. The abuse
continued. It was foul and aggressive, followed by sick
laughter. I had to respond. Choking with anger, I set my
resolve.

'No, actually you're wrong,' I called out, as calmly as
I could manage. 'Jesus is alive. I know that because he's
living in my heart, so I'm going to forgive you. God bless
you, OK?'

There was a moment's silence. Then I realised what
was about to happen. I stood still, bowed my head and
recited Psalm 23 to myself . . .

> Even though I walk through the valley of the shadow of
> death,
> I will fear no evil, for you are with me . . .

Boiling hot water came teaming out from the upper
window. I braced myself as the water hit. Steam rose off
my clothes, yet somehow the water felt cool, refreshing
even. There was not a burn on me. I stood in disbelief,
then called out to the man.

'Oi, you, come to the window.' There was a roar of
laughter.

'What are you, chicken?' I shouted. Silence. I thought
what to do, then called up to him. 'I want you to know
this, whoever you are. I'm not a grass, so I'm not going
to grass you up. I'm not even going to come looking for
you. If I wasn't a Christian I'd beat your brains out, but
I love Jesus too much for that. I'm here because I've done
some bad things and I'm ashamed.' No sound came
from upstairs. I continued. 'I want you to know I forgive

you in the name of the Lord Jesus Christ. God bless you.'

Many of the other men saw and heard what was happening. 'You've got to sort him out, Tony,' they said. 'Tell us which room it came from and we'll get him for you.'

'No, I'm not going to do that,' I replied. They thought I was crazy. By the time I got back into the block, a couple of the guards had heard about what had happened.

'Tell us who it was Tony, we'll do something about it,' they said.

'No, I'm not going to grass him up. I told him I wouldn't.'

'But you can't let him get away with that,' they said. One of them caught me by the arm and spoke quietly. 'Look, we'll turn a blind eye. Go upstairs and give him the kicking he deserves. We'll come in a few minutes later and help you.'

'You know I can't do that,' I said. 'My ways have changed now.' The officers were dumbstruck. I tried to explain. 'Look, I want to forgive this man. The power of forgiveness brings freedom. It is a much more powerful thing than retaliation.' I told them about the ancient times of jubilee when the lords and kings would set all the prisoners free and cancel all debt. 'To know Jesus Christ is like this,' I said. 'It is a time of jubilee, of celebration and rejoicing. To know his forgiveness brings true freedom and happiness into people's lives. Hatred is a lifelong prison. I know I need to forgive this man, whoever he is.' The officers looked at each other and shrugged their shoulders. One patted me on the back.

'You're a better man than me, Pastor,' he smiled.

I never did retaliate, but I heard later that some of my friends from the ground floor had worked out where the water had come from. In the next open time a group of them had gone upstairs and dealt a heavy warning to my aggressor. I never had any trouble from him again.

Chapter 16

The chapel was always a good place to hang out. Men went there as an excuse to get out of their cells. The Church of England chaplain didn't have much of a heart for the gospel. He was a weary chap who'd worked at the prison for years. Each evening he left for the outside world, but he was just as much a captive as any of us locked in the cells. My sharing the gospel clearly irritated him, but there was little he could do about it.

Week by week men were becoming Christians and we gathered regularly in the chapel to talk, study and pray. There were several onlookers. Sometimes they joined in. Beau Beasley was one of them. He was a young man, an addict, with pale skin and a haunted look in his eyes. He'd spent most of his adult life in prison. 'It's no good me being on the outside,' he confided in me one day. Each time his sentence was nearly up, Beau would cause just enough trouble to ensure he lost his remand. 'This is my home,' he told me. 'Outside it's hard. There's no one for me out there. I have to pay bills and find somewhere to live. Who needs the worry? At least in here I get hot meals and I'm with my mates.' There were too many men like Beau.

Swampy was another character who hung around the chapel. Outside he'd enjoyed national press coverage through his anarchistic environmental endeavours. Inside, he was something of a loner. Few cared about saving trees and fields in Bullingdon. He was heavily involved in paganism and would often have his

233

'priestess' come to the chapel to visit him. She became involved with the chaplain and even started running some of the Church of England services on Sundays. It infuriated me. All I could do was pray. Sure enough, God intervened and, for some reason, I don't know what, she was stopped from visiting.

Swampy came storming up to me. Pushing me purposefully he said, 'Oi, I've heard about you and your devious stuff, praying to get my priestess thrown out. When you're not looking I'm gonna have the back of your head.' I firmly took his hand off my shoulder. He was a good deal taller than me, but I pushed my face close up to his.

'Now you listen to me,' I said. 'You do what you've got to do. If you want to do it right now, I'll turn around and you can take a hit,' I said, through clenched teeth. 'But know this,' I continued. 'Whatever you do, I'm going to forgive you. I love you in the name of Jesus Christ. I mean you no harm, but you go ahead. Do what you've got to do.' Swampy stood glaring at me. Neither of us knew what should happen next. Finally, he swore and walked off.

Six months went by and I was told to prepare myself for release. I didn't know what was ahead of me but God had taught me so much. I was a different man. Sara, too, had grown in her relationship with God. She'd come to depend on him much more and, like me, was spending more time in prayer. Life wasn't easy for her and Ethan, but my heart warmed when I heard her talk, in a new way, about her love for Jesus.

By 12 February 2002, my release date, I'd saved up a good amount of money. I wanted to make one final gesture to the men I had got to know over the months. I walked into the chapel, where the usual crowd and a few others had gathered. 'What's in the bag, Pastor?' asked

Sam Paul, the guy who'd first given me my nickname (I called him 'Hagrid'). I tipped it up on the table and a shower of Mars bars came cascading out.

'There's one for everyone,' I shouted above the laughter. Mars bars were a big deal among the prisoners, especially those who used all their money on cigarettes. 'Look guys, it's my last day here. As you know, I don't smoke, so I've saved up my wages to get you a little something to remember me by. This is my way of saying, "God bless you."'

I walked around the chapel, making sure that everyone got a chocolate bar. I was pleased to see Swampy was there. He looked a little sheepish. Among the Christians it had become something of a tradition that we would all stand in a circle and say the grace to one another:

> May the grace of our Lord Jesus Christ, the love of God and the fellowship of the Holy Spirit be with us all, evermore. Amen.

As we did this, I surveyed the room. There were a good number of men who I knew had been radically changed in the last few months. Swampy stood in the circle, too. He didn't say the grace, but he smiled. He came to me and put out a fist of friendship. I put my fist to his. 'You're alright, mate,' he said. 'God bless you,' I smiled.

I continued to write to Swampy and many of the other men after my release. Letters came flooding back and today I find myself with a continuing ministry, supporting and encouraging many of them. Some have since been released. Others have moved to different prisons and I try to visit as much as possible.

Of all the lives transformed during those six months, there was none more so than mine. Looking back over the time since the accident, I recognised that God had allowed me to fall into the wilderness. Only there could he do a work in me. Only there could he deal with my arrogance, my zealot nature. Only there could he bring me to my knees and teach me humility, a lesson I so badly needed to learn.

As I studied my Bible I realised that many of God's chosen people had endured wilderness experiences. Some had literally been drawn into the desert. Moses and the children of Israel, after their dramatic release from slavery, spent forty years there. I read their story in Deuteronomy chapter 8 and a key verse stood out:

> Remember how the Lord your God led you all the way in the desert these forty years, to humble you and to test you in order to know what was in your heart, whether or not you would keep his commands . . .

I realised that, like me, the children of Israel had sinned again and again. They let God down, even after they had seen great and mighty things. Still, God loved them. I read on and discovered that he provided them with water, food, shoes and clothing that didn't wear out. He had a plan for them. Eventually he spoke to them, giving Israel a new revelation: the Ten Commandments.

As I leafed through the Bible stories I discovered that, time and again, the most pivotal events took place through wilderness experiences. I dug into my study Bible and was fascinated to discover that one of the Hebrew words for 'wilderness' actually translates as 'the place where God speaks'.

I was hungry to find out more. I knew that John the Baptist was referred to as 'a voice calling from the wilderness'. When I studied his character, I discovered more about what God wanted me to be. John's ministry,

in human terms, was a huge success. Many responded to
his message and people queued up to be baptised. He
was the kind of evangelist I dreamed of being. John
knew, however, that he himself was not the focus of his
message. His purpose was to prepare the way for the
coming Messiah. I read the Gospel of John and noted
chapter 3 verse 30 where John said of Jesus, 'He must
become greater; I must become less.'

The more I pondered all this, the more my fascination
grew. Even Jesus, I read, was led by the Holy Spirit into
the desert. He stayed there forty days and forty nights
and, three times, he was tempted by the devil. Unlike
many of the other people in the Bible, Jesus was able to
be perfectly obedient to his Father. He did not get caught
up in the temptations of the world. 'Jesus is the ultimate
role model,' I reflected.

I relished the time Bullingdon afforded me to study
and discover more about him. Whilst he had the strength
to fight the temptations of the desert, he was still the
ultimate picture of humility. Broken in both body and
spirit, he carried the sins of mankind as he died on the
cross. I found myself looking back into the Old
Testament to see what the prophets foretold about him.
In Psalm 22 I found prophetic words of Jesus himself.
Verse 6 gave me a picture that really struck home
through my understanding of Kung Fu and the animals
I had mimicked. 'I am a worm and not a man,' said Jesus.
I remembered my training in the way of the snake.
Under attack, the snake rears itself up, hisses and strikes
back. It is a true picture of self. A worm, on the other
hand, offers no resistance. It allows you to do what you
like with it, kick it or squash it under your heel. It is a
picture of true brokenness.

I sat for a long time, mulling over this image. Jesus,
the Son of God, the creator of all, was willing to become

broken, like a worm, for me. How much more should I be broken for him? He was not looking for a perfect Christian, neatly packaged in respectable wrapping. I realised that was what I had been striving to become. I had got caught up in the temptations of middle class life, my job, our mortgage, a better car. I remembered Jesus' words from the parable of the sower, recorded in Mark 4:19: ' . . . but the worries of this life, the deceitfulness of wealth and the desires for other things come in and choke the word, making it unfruitful.' There is nothing wrong with having a nice home and good things, I reasoned. I knew that Jesus' teaching here was dealing more with my attitude towards them. Without even realising it, the 'good life' had become my goal. My loyalties lay with the pursuit of earthly things, not the pursuit of God.

From the early days since I had become a Christian I had studied the teaching of the apostle Paul. He was a man I could truly relate to. Like me, Paul was a sinner of gigantic proportion. Like me, he had experienced Jesus in a very dramatic way. Like me, he was physically imprisoned. Paul described himself as 'in chains' for the 'mystery of Christ' (Colossians 4:3). I gazed out through the window at the men walking in the courtyard. Some were proud of their criminal endeavours. Others, like me, were ashamed and repentant. Either way, I reflected, they are all prisoners of self. How I longed for each one of them to know the saving grace of Christ Jesus.

I often scribbled down thoughts, or simply doodled with a pencil and paper as I meditated on Scripture. I looked at my pad and realised that I'd jotted down a Cantonese character. I smiled, recognising it to be 'Yi', the word for 'righteousness'. Yi, in Cantonese script, is formed by placing the character for 'lamb' (Yang) above the character for the pronoun 'I' (Wo). In the Gospel of John, Jesus is referred to as the 'Lamb of God who takes away the sin of the world' (John 1:29). What an appropriate symbol for the righteousness God offers sinners through faith in Christ!

Throughout my time in Bullingdon I prayed that God would prepare a way ahead for me. There was plenty to be concerned about. I wondered about my relationship with Sara and Ethan. She had learned to live without a husband. He had never really known me as a father. How would I fit in with their lives? Sara had found us a house, but I needed a job to help pay the way. Who would employ me with my record?

Above all, I knew that I didn't want to go back to being the kind of Christian I had become before my time in prison. I prayed that I would be able to continue God's work, witnessing for him and evangelising. But this time it needed to be different. 'Please God, surround me with a team of people who can support me and keep me living in humility and brokenness before you,' I prayed.

God answered my prayers in all areas, and in his timing. Within days of my release, Sara told me it was as though I had never been away. She was different. Like me, she had been brought to her knees before Jesus. There were stickers with Bible verses on the fridge and all around the house. Ethan adjusted well. We played rough and laughed together. My heart brimmed over with joy every time he yelled 'Daddy' and launched himself into my arms. I had so much to learn from him.

By the end of that first week I'd secured a job, waiting on tables in a restaurant. I was honest with the manager about where I'd spent the past six months. He was still happy to take me on. The pay was lousy, but each day I made sure I turned up at work with a smile on my face.

It was an important witness that came very naturally. I was full of a new joy. God is a God of second chances, and that truth shone out from me. My old aggression had gone and I felt as though Jesus was showing me new things. I seemed to be able to see beneath people's masks. There were many hurting people and I longed to reach out to each one of them. Often, on the bus, or in the restaurant, I would find myself talking to someone about Jesus, with a new boldness. It didn't matter if I made a fool of myself. I had let God down many times, but he was not ashamed of me, how could I be ashamed of him?

With that attitude, I wasn't afraid to share my faith with anyone. At the same time I learned to recognise God's heart for people. Not everyone I met needed the gospel to be shoved down their throat. Sometimes they just needed a smile, or a listening ear. Sometimes I handed them some Bible-based literature or a summary of my testimony that I'd prepared. I always included my telephone number and a simple invitation to contact me. I was amazed how many phone calls I received. 'You spoke to me on the bus today . . . ' or 'We met a few weeks ago in the supermarket queue . . . ' There were people who had been raised in faith, or those who had made a commitment to God but had fallen away. There were others who had never come across anyone talking about God in such a personal way. Many people got in touch with me simply because they wanted a listening ear to spill out their problems to.

In the meantime, I committed myself to humble service in our church. The people at Leigh Road Baptist Church had been hugely supportive to both Sarah and me throughout my time in Bullingdon. They welcomed me back with loving arms. I was eager to get involved with evangelism but I hung on to God's promise for me. As the time of my release from prison had drawn near I had been convicted by a passage in the first chapter of the book of Acts. Jesus had appeared to his followers after his death and they were eager to know of his plan for them. He instructed them to wait in Jerusalem until they were given a gift from his Father. That is what I believed God was telling me: 'Wait until the time is right.'

Revd Steven Hembery was very understanding and supportive. He knew of the experience I'd had working among young people and encouraged me to help out with the local youth work and missions. He also invited me to share my testimony with the church. I had so much to tell. I split my story into two parts, spreading the talks a good six months or so apart. Both events were met with very emotional responses. Everyone was amazed at the story of my early life and my first encounter with God. Few people in this world can relate to my life of Kung Fu and violence, but there were people at the church who, through my story, became convinced of the reality of Jesus Christ for the first time. There was much celebration that day.

The most overwhelming response was yet to come. Many of the congregation had been Christians for years. Some had fallen into the same trap I had before the accident. They had become comfortable and unchallenged in their faith. They had lost their passion for Jesus and their drive to tell others about him. I knew only too well that many of the people sitting before me were good, honest folk who worked hard for their church, and genuinely loved one another. 'But are you really broken to the will of God?' I asked them. 'Or are you working in your own self-righteousness and your own strength, the way that I'd been doing?' I highlighted the apostle Paul's teaching in Galatians 2:20: ' . . . I no longer live, but Christ lives in me.'

'I have come to realise,' I told my friends, 'that Jesus cannot live in me fully and reveal himself through me until my proud "self" within is broken. It is a hard, unyielding self,' I continued. 'It justifies itself, it wants its own way, it stands up for its rights and seeks its own glory,' I preached. 'Until that self finally bows its head to God's will, admits it is wrong and gives up its own way to Jesus, he will never be able to break into your life and use you for his will. You will never know the true joy of living in him, rather than through your own selfish desires.' A silent hush fell over the church.

I went on to talk more about my 'wilderness' experience, knowing that many in the congregation would relate only too well. They didn't have to be behind prison bars to feel deserted, alone and floundering before God. Sharing my experience, I was able to encourage them: 'God does his business with his people in the wilderness. When all else is lost, his still small voice can be heard calling in the desert. Don't be afraid of suffering,' I told them. 'Suffering and testing will come, but here is your opportunity to demonstrate your trust in God and your obedience to him. Be still. Know that he is the God who loves you and will provide for you. He knows what he is doing in your life. Take time to listen to him, to discover his perfect ways.'

As the meeting drew to a close many people were moved to tears, none more so than me. An old lady approached me. Her face shone with the love of Jesus. She thanked me for my message. Then she gave me a warning. 'You have been through a long and deep wilderness,' she said. 'But don't imagine that God will not lead you into this place again.' I shivered. It was not what I had expected to hear. 'Be vigilant. Stay close to him,' she said. With that she was gone. It was a message that I keep close to my heart. In its light, I surrender myself to Jesus every single day, knowing that his work in me has only just begun.

In the last few years I have told my story in churches, schools, old people's homes, on the street, in prisons, sports halls and in many kinds of meetings up and down the UK. God continues to answer my prayer and to use me to share the good news about Jesus Christ.

My story is a message for all people, because it is God's message: that of a broken man made whole, a wicked man forgiven, a life restored, made new and filled with joy for the present and hope for the future. I pray that you will take this story and make it your own.

Afterword (about the authors)

In 2003, Tony Anthony, with the support of a team of directors, established Avanti Ministries Limited. 'Avanti' is the Italian word for 'Go', and the organisation's name is derived from Jesus' Great Commission:

> Therefore go and make disciples of all nations, baptising them in the name of the Father and of the Son and of the Holy Spirit, and teaching them to obey everything I have commanded you. And surely I am with you always, to the very end of the age. (Matthew 28:19,20)

Avanti's mission is to work in alliance with local churches, helping them to communicate the good news of Jesus Christ in their community.

In early 2004, Tony committed himself to full time evangelism and currently manages a busy itinerary. From schools to old people's homes, prisons to cinemas and out on the streets, he finds himself telling his story and sharing the gospel, both at home and internationally. With the support of a committed and experienced team he organises youth events, family 'fun days' and all manner of small to large-scale outreach missions. Avanti's emphasis is on equipping local churches to take the gospel message directly to the world, with urgency and, above all, relevance. The team specialises in teaching and training, running evangelism and discipleship courses for all levels, challenging the church towards growth and maturity.

Tony continues to support many of the inmates in HMP Bullingdon (including some mentioned in this book who have since completed their sentences) and also inmates of other prisons around the UK.

Tony and Sara still live in Essex, with their two sons, Ethan and Jacob.

Angela Little is a freelance writer. A former Editor of *Premier* magazine, she has collaborated on a number of titles published through Authentic Media and Hodder & Stoughton. She currently lives in Northamptonshire with husband, Phil, and young son, Samuel.

For more information about Avanti, visit the website: www.avantiministries.com or contact Tony direct by email: tony@avantiministries.com